C000057031

EPHESUS

to

LAODICEA

A Study Guide
to the
Seven Churches in
the Book of Revelation

Clifford and Monica Hill

British Library Cataloguing in Publication Data:
A catalogue record for this publication
is available from the British Library

ISBN   1 871828 65 1

(from 2007: 978 1 871828 65 8)

© **The Handsel Press 2005**
CD-rom © John Law 2005

Typeset in 11 pt. Garamond

Printed by Polestar Wheaton, Exeter

Distributed by C & M Ministries, Moggerhanger Park MK44 3RW

CONTENTS

CD Rom inside the back cover , contents and instructions opposite

WESTERN TURKEY TODAY, MODERN PLACE NAMES

PREFACE

How the Study Guide came to be written

Turkey is a late comer onto the tourist scene. It is only in recent years that tour operators have discovered the beaches and historical sites that make it an attractive holiday destination for those seeking sun and sand as well as an exploration of archaeological treasures. Since the 1980s hotels, particularly along the West Coast, have sprung up in large numbers to accommodate the increasing numbers of package holidays on offer.

Turkey is attractive not only to European sun worshippers but it holds an attraction for Christian pilgrims almost on a par with Israel. The attraction is the sites of the Seven Churches addressed in the Book of Revelation, the last book in the Bible, and one that has for centuries held a fascination for Christians, especially those who study eschatology - the Bible's teaching on the 'last days' or the end of the world.

We made our first visit to the Seven Churches before they were discovered by tour operators, when it was difficult to find a local guide who knew where to find some of the sites. On that first visit our guide was unable to locate Laodicea and with the aid of local maps, both ancient and modern, we were able to point him in the right general direction. But it was not until our second visit, following a lot of research, that we were able to get our party to the right site.

We were subsequently asked by MasterSun, a Christian tour operator, to help train a party of their staff by taking them around the circuit travelled by the original messenger whom the Apostle John dispatched from Patmos. It was at this point that we realised the need for a study guidebook that would be both historically accurate and practical to help the modern visitor to understand what they are seeing. Bob and Jill Fleming encouraged us to write such a book as, apart from commentaries on the biblical text, there was no publication that met the need.

We started writing the present book about ten years ago but due to many other pressures of ministry it was never finished. It was one of those things that we kept saying to ourselves we really should make a priority but it was left on the back burner. Following requests from a number of different sources we made a big effort in 2004 to complete the text. Then we felt the need to check its accuracy and relevance and make sure that it really was helpful to visitors. We invited some of our ministry supporters to come with us on a specially arranged tour, each armed with a copy of the draft manuscript and invited to take part in a critical appraisal.

Growing popularity of visiting the Seven Churches

It is not only British people, Europeans and Americans who are going to explore the sites of the Seven Churches. Christians from around the world, especially from Korea and Japan are visiting in increasing numbers. In each of the cities addressed in Revelation chapters two and three they read the letter to that church, spend time in prayer and seek to understand the relevance of its message for their own situation. Of course, the ease of travel today enables people to visit places of which they could only read a generation or so ago. But the growing popularity of the Seven Churches of Revelation as a pilgrimage for Christians is of greater significance than a mere interest in archaeological remains.

It is a unique experience to sit on the stone steps of the great theatre in Ephesus. You can almost hear Paul arguing with his companions who scarcely restrained him from trying to speak to the mob that had been stirred up by Demetrius and his fellow craftsmen. The latter feared for their trade in the artefacts of Artemis as increasing numbers responded to the gospel which Paul preached in the city. A few hundred yards from the theatre you can sit in the chancel of the Church of St Mary the Virgin where the important Council of Ephesus was held, and you can stand in what is probably the oldest baptistry in the world. At Philadelphia you can stand in awe of the great pillars of one of the oldest church buildings, the former Roman Town Hall; or in Sardis you can visit the little shops once owned by Christians alongside the great synagogue. In each place you know that you are standing where brothers and sisters in Christ witnessed to their faith in the earliest days of Christianity. They were days of great danger and uncertainty for believers in Jesus as wave after wave of persecution swept the Roman Empire.

Ancient ruins: Modern message

There is something special about actually being in these places that is much more than the attraction of standing among the ruins of beautiful architecture. It is the search for a spiritual experience that draws Christians to these ancient sites. There is a growing conviction among Christians that the messages addressed to the believers in the Seven Churches of Asia Minor in the first century of the Christian era have a special relevance for the followers of Jesus twenty centuries later.

The bewildering speed of both social and technological change in the second half of the twentieth century and the early years of the twenty-first century have created a universal sense of unease and uncertainty for the future. The great wars of the twentieth century left millions dead on the battlefield and in the bombed ruins of once thriving cities. The Communist empire dominated by Soviet Russia through most of the 20th century brought misery to millions and severe persecution to Christians.

The collapse of the USSR in 1990 coincided with the rise of a new phase of Islam with its hatred of the West and persecution of Jews and Christians. At the same time the Western nations have been experiencing the bitter fruit of their spiritual apostasy and rejection of their Judaeo/Christian biblical heritage, seen in the breakdown of family life and personal morality. All these things have combined to produce the sense of unease and fear for the future that is felt in every nation today.

This is the background to the growing popularity among Christians from many nations of undertaking a tour from Ephesus to Laodicea. They are seeking much more than a holiday in the sun or a walk around ancient ruins. They come for a spiritual pilgrimage that will enable them to make sense of the modern world by understanding what God said to his people at the beginning of the Christian era. Just being in the places where the first generation of Christians after Pentecost stood firm in their faith in the face of the might of the Roman legions helps to bring alive part of the Bible where the experience of believers appears to have some affinity with our modern world.

Relevance for today

The messages to the churches of Ephesus, Smyrna, Pergamum, Thyatira, Sardis, Philadelphia and Laodicea contain warnings, exhortations and words of encouragement for believers in Jesus. The warnings were largely concerning the dangers of straying from the true faith through the lure of alternative teaching, or the attraction of the world. Similar dangers are facing us today, often in a subtle form, due to the sophistication of modern civilisation and the wealth and comfort that surrounds us today.

The exhortations were to stand firm in the faith despite the fierce opposition to the gospel by the authorities and the treachery of friends and neighbours who sometimes denounced Christians as part of personal vendettas. For Christians today persecution is a present reality in many parts of the world. Some 200,000 Christians are being killed every year, largely by fanatical Muslims, but also by militant Buddhists in Sri Lanka, Communists in China, and Hindus in India. In the West, opposition to the gospel from secular authorities is growing as the onslaught of secularism gathers momentum. We are, perhaps, nearer to actual persecution in many western nations than most Christians realise.

The words of encouragement to the first century Christians were climaxed in beautiful promises to the 'overcomers', to those who put their loyalty to Jesus above everything and whose lives were filled with love, joy and peace. These same words of encouragement come to us today with freshness and clarity through the ministry of the Holy Spirit.

This is the attraction of following in the footsteps of the messenger from Patmos as he made the long journey by foot from Ephesus to Laodicea. We can do this same journey today in the comfort of an air-conditioned bus, carrying in our hands the same letters as John sent to the groups of Christians meeting in each of the seven cities. But this study guide can also be useful to enable those who are unable to travel to Turkey to have a vicarious 'reality' experience. Through the combined use of the CD, the study-guide and the Bible, the message to the Seven Churches of Revelation can come alive today.

The study guide is especially designed to help those who wish to undertake a journey of faith with a desire in their hearts to gain fresh understanding of an important part of the message of the Book of Revelation. Through this understanding God can speak into the lives of his people and into the situations in which they are working out their personal discipleship.

Clifford and Monica Hill
September 2005
Moggerhanger Park
Bedford

ACKNOWLEDGMENTS

Forty-three modern 'pilgrims', all keen to undertake a 'working-holiday', set off for Turkey intent on re-discovering part of ancient Asia Minor in April 2005. Each went armed with a copy of the draft manuscript of this study-guide, determined to check it for accuracy and relevance.

A number of those who undertook the tour from Ephesus to Laodicea had already spent many hours of preparation prior to meeting at Gatwick airport. Others could be seen hastily reading the manuscript during the flight! But all joined enthusiastically in the exploration of the sites and the discussion of their impressions and experiences at the group meetings each evening.

Members of the group came from all parts of the UK (and we even had one from Switzerland); from Anglesey in the West to Ipswich in the East; from the Isle of Wight in the South to Scotland in the North. The common denominator was that they were supporters and prayer partners of our ministry at Moggerhanger Park. They were a very special group with a wide variety of gifts and expertise who rapidly became a task-orientated, praying, worshiping community enjoying shared spiritual experiences and wonderful fun and relaxation together.

Those who were part of the group, all of whom have contributed insights and contributions to this study-guide, were: -

Mr Gordon Brown	Dr John Law
Mr and Mrs David & Joyce Brown	Miss Amy Law
Mr and Mrs Rob & Sylvia Darby	Revd and Mrs John & Monica Lewis
Mrs Rosemary Darrington	Revd and Mrs Ron & Joyce Lycett
Mrs Patricia Davies-Griffith	Mr and Mrs Brian & Mary Newsom
Mrs Anne Garner	Revd Gillian Orpin
Mrs Jane Ghosh	Mr and Mrs Keith & Rosemary Pavitt
Mrs Joyce Giles	Dr Robert & Dr Valerie Rowe
Mr and Mrs John & Jennifer Godfrey	Mrs Rosina Sharp
Mrs Karen Goodman	Revd Jock & Revd Margaret Stein
Revd and Mrs Malcolm & Jean Guest	Miss Ros Turner
Miss Pamela Hewitt	Revd Michael Wieteska
Revd Dr Clifford & Mrs Monica Hill	Mrs Barbara Wood
Mrs Dorothy Horsman	Mrs Brenda Woodward
Miss Kathleen Horton	Revd Jenny Yates
Dr and Mrs Ivan & Margaret Howcroft	

The worship and sharing times at the end of each day were special; so too were the times of worship and prayer on the bus. Special thanks to worship leaders - Ros, Jenny, Jock, Pamela and Joyce.

With so many ministers, academics and theologians in the group the sharing times at each site and in the evenings were of a high quality, but we want to acknowledge and thank every one of the group whose spiritual insights and observations contributed much to this study-guide. Our special thanks go to:

Jock Stein of Handsel Press who prepared the final manuscript for the printer and dealt with all the practical issues of publication

John Law – a great photographer who took all the photos and edited the production of the CD and PowerPoint presentation... and to the volunteers who put the CDs in the back of the book

David Brown – who made a video and added his personal reflections

Margaret Stein – an exceptional artist whose drawings are included in the text

Monica Lewis - a cartographer who took responsibility for the maps

Robert Rowe and Rob Darby and the other academics, clergy and scholars who contributed their expertise and insights

Rosina Sharp whose contacts with Turkish believers enriched our fellowship

Barbara Wood for bringing a pedometer to measure how far we walked!!

Ros Turner – whose youthful enthusiasm marks her as an outstanding leader of the future!

Michael Wieteska from Geneva for allowing us to use his home in North Wales to edit the manuscript and incorporate the many comments and insights from the group

Yalçin Dogulu – 'John' – our guide from Izmir, renowned to be the best guide in Turkey – who greatly contributed to our understanding of the sites.

We are especially grateful to Bob and Jill Fleming of MasterSun, who encouraged us to write this book and made all the practical arrangements for the tour.

We are also grateful to Jocelyn Pimm of Worldwide Christian Travel who hosted some of our earlier visits.

Our gratitude goes to Rob Danby and Dorothy Richards (who had been with us before) who helped us keep to the timetable on proof editing.

Our thanks are due to the trustees of C&M Ministries, our personal support group, who underwrote the whole venture – and have covered the costs.

We are also grateful for all the love and support we receive from our colleagues in all the ministries at Moggerhanger who work and pray together as a family.

Finally our thanks are due to all our prayer partners who have been so supportive and prayed consistently (and patiently) for the completion of this book.

And, of course, our greatest thanks are to God for all his goodness and protection on the journey and for making this publication possible.

Clifford and Monica Hill

The CD Rom and Copyright

The CD at the back of this book contains many beautiful photographs that prepare the way for the pilgrim who takes the road from Ephesus to Laodicea. In providing this preview the CD enables Christians to know where to look for things that are of the greatest significance. They can be freely reproduced for personal use or for use in home groups or local churches. They are, however, protected by copyright in the case of commercial use. Permission needs to be sought from the publishers for any such use.

The CD also contains two PowerPoint presentations which will be particularly useful to those who have undertaken the journey around Turkey and wish to help their friends back home to enter into some of that experience. Notes are provided with each slide so that the presenter can be armed with prompt-notes and teaching material to bring the pictures alive for those who have not had first-hand exposure to the sites of the Seven Churches.

It is hoped that the notes, together with the main text in the study guide, will provide material that will stimulate further study and discussion of these fascinating messages to the Seven Churches. The writers, and all those who have contributed to this study guide, trust that it will both inform and bless many, enabling them to be effective witnesses in the twenty-first century world and to join the great company of the 'overcomers', the first of whom were gathered into the Kingdom from Ephesus to Laodicea twenty centuries ago.

Pergamum

.Thyatira

Smyrna   Sardis

Philadelphia

Ephesus   .Laodicea

Patmos

100 Km

········> Route taken by
John's messenger
to the Seven Churches

THE SEVEN CHURCHES IN ASIA MINOR, 90AD

Part 1 Background and Introduction

Chapter 1

History of the Region

Modern-day Turkey, which was once part of the Greek Empire, is sometimes said to have the greatest collection of Greek archaeological remains in the world (possibly even more than modern Greece!) which acts as a magnet for an increasing number of visitors. They come in historic tour parties and on cruise liners to clamber over the ruins of by-gone civilisations, and to look at the tangible evidence of events and places that former generations were only able to read about in their history books. Christians also come in biblical tour parties because the region has great significance as an area of intense missionary activity in apostolic times.

Today, the ease of modern travel has made western Turkey popular with tourists who are attracted to its unique mixture of classical archaeological sites, natural beauty, excellent beaches and a warm sunny climate. Two of the Seven Wonders of the Ancient World are located in this area - the Mausoleum at Halicarnassus and the Artemisium (Temple) at Ephesus. Most of the Greek place-names have been changed since Turkey was founded as a modern state in 1922.

Hundreds of thousands of visitors from all over Europe explore the ruins of ancient temples and archaeological excavations in places such as Troy, Bodrum (Halicarnassus), Priene, Sart (Sardis), Pamukkale (Hierapolis), Selcuk (Ephesus) and Bergama (Pergamum). An increasing number of visitors are discovering for themselves unrevealed and unexcavated ancient sites. Many of them are being plundered before the money can be raised to allow them to be properly excavated.

The Christian visitor views the sites of the temples of these classical gods and goddesses as part of the historical and spiritual background to the first century AD mission of the apostles. Both Paul and John were known to have laboured in this region of the Roman Empire and the information given in Acts plus some of Paul's letters and the message to the Seven Churches make it an area of special pilgrimage and spiritual significance for Christians. A visit here helps to bring the New Testament alive for the Christian today.

The earliest record of life in this region was provided by Homer who was probably born in Smyrna (modern Izmir) in the eighth century BC. His historical record of events in the region was based on folk-lore passed down by word of mouth through tribal communities. This folk-lore kept alive the memory of events leading up to the Greek siege of Troy and the subsequent disintegration of the Mycenaean civilisation which had taken place some 500 years earlier at the close of the Bronze Age (c.1200 BC).

The Anatolian to Hellenistic Periods

Some two centuries later following the invasion of Greece by the Dorians, there was a large-scale population movement from the Greek mainland eastward into the islands off the Aegean coast and the coastal plain of Anatolia. First to come were the Aeolians (around the eleventh century BC) who settled in the northern area around Troy and as far south as Smyrna. Next came the Ionians who settled in the middle region around Ephesus. Finally the Dorians themselves (around the tenth century BC) moved into the southern area around Halicarnassus, the modern Bodrum.

Each group of settlers maintained their Greek identity and culture including the Dorians who by this time had become thoroughly Hellenized. Each of these groups founded a number of cities that were linked together by culture for commerce and defence such as the Dodecapolis in the Ionian region. These were called 'Leagues'. And each group sent out expeditions to establish colonies in centres all over the Mediterranean world (Miletus alone founded some 80 colonies). This resulted in the spread of the Greek culture and learning, thus beginning the Hellenization which was to have a lasting influence upon world history.

Many of the earliest and greatest Greek poets, philosophers, sculptors, painters, architects, city planners, physicists, physicians, mathematicians, astronomers, geographers and historians came from the Ionic region of Anatolia or modern day Turkey. The cities in the whole of the Aegean region changed hands many times in the period down to the beginning of the Christian era but never lost their Greek identity and culture, even surviving the centuries of Lydian, Persian, Macedonian and Roman occupation. Sometimes they were given favoured status, such as Pergamum which became an important independent state under Persia, but more often their cities and beautiful buildings were burnt, ransacked and destroyed and needed to be rebuilt and sometimes re-sited as successive invaders took control.

The Roman Period

The region became the Roman province of Asia (or Asia Minor) from 129 BC and the Romans concentrated their provincial government and military power along the coastal strip of the Aegean from which they were able to control the inland regions. In recognition of its importance as a centre of commerce and travel the port of Ephesus was upgraded by Augustus to become the capital of the province, replacing Pergamum which was more inland. The Romans, however, respected the Greek culture and unlike earlier or later conquerors they did not destroy the great temples, theatres or classical buildings but adapted some, modified others and added many more. New buildings included the Temples of Domitian and Hadrian and the Celsus Library in Ephesus, the Temple of Dionysus and the Trajaneum at Pergamum and the completion of the Temple to Artemis at Sardis.

The Romans were still in control at the time of Jesus and although they tolerated Christianity at first, this situation changed as the new religion grew and was perceived as a threat to the political unity of the Empire. The first widespread persecution had just begun when the letters to the Seven Churches were written.

At the end of the first century it is thought that there were at least 500 churches in the region – some of them bigger than the Seven addressed in the Revelation given to John. The gospel spread rapidly throughout the region during the Apostolic period and by the middle of the first century it was already presenting a serious threat to the pagan religions. There is good evidence for this in Luke's account of Paul's mission in Asia. He says that 'all the Jews and Greeks who lived in the province of Asia heard the word of the Lord' (Acts 19:10).

The Apostolic Period

The extraordinary success of Paul's preaching and church planting is glimpsed in the little incidents recorded by Luke such as the events in Ephesus that led up to the riot initiated by Demetrius the silversmith. Luke records, 'a number who had practised sorcery brought their scrolls together and burnt them publicly. When they calculated the value of the scrolls, the total came to 50,000 drachmas. In this way the word of the Lord spread widely and grew in power' (Acts 19:19-20).

The success of the gospel and the spread of Christianity was a serious threat to the traditional religions and sparked the kind of fierce opposition that was seen in Ephesus where the silversmiths were afraid that the craftsmen and related trades would lose their business as people rejected the worship of the goddess Artemis (Diana) and put their faith in Jesus. Christianity was a threat to all the religions of the region including the imperial cult of emperor worship which until the advent of Christianity was the most popular system of religion incorporating 'Dominus et Deus'.

The Jews, although having enjoyed a period of privileged status for a number of years in many areas under Roman rule, were highly unpopular and had actually been banished from Rome for a period of about 10 years by Claudius in AD 45. We know that there were constant arguments between Hebraic Jews and Messianics (Jewish converts to Christianity) and these sometimes became violent and spilled over into the streets from the synagogue and thereby came to the attention of the authorities. The Christians were seen to be a sect of Judaism and it is no doubt this connection that led to them being regarded as troublemakers and an easy target for mob violence when a scapegoat was sought.

The persecution in Rome in the decade of the 60s initiated by Nero is generally believed to have been due to his need to re-impose the supremacy of emperor worship as well as being aimed at Christians in his desire to find a scapegoat following the disastrous fire in that city.

Spread of the Gospel

Elsewhere in the Empire the gospel was making rapid inroads into the social composition of the population with large numbers embracing the new faith. It is, nevertheless, difficult to see why Rome should initiate any official suppression of Christianity which could hardly have been regarded as a threat to the security of the Empire. Its message was one of *spiritual* salvation, not of social revolution. The gospel was presented as offering a new and intimate relationship with God the Creator through the forgiveness of sins. Those who responded were known as followers of 'the Way'. They represented a new way of life and were exhorted to love one another and even to love their enemies because they were citizens of a heavenly kingdom whose architect and builder was God. This hardly represented political sedition.

There is no suggestion either in New Testament literature or in any other source that Christianity was regarded as a popular people's liberation movement. Equally there is no evidence that the Roman authorities feared the spread of Christianity on the grounds that it presented a political threat. There were other grounds on which the Romans feared for the unity of the Empire. These will be examined later.

According to Tertullian, Nero was the first to introduce restrictive or oppressive measures against Christians and he had his own personal reasons for this (see Chapter 2). It is probable that both Peter and Paul lost their lives at this time.

Persecution

The persecution initiated by Nero was mercifully brief and confined to the area around Rome but a much more serious and widespread persecution took place during the reign of Domitian (AD 81 - 96) in the two years before his assassination at the hands of Stephanus. Christians had gradually begun to be regarded as suspect particularly because they were intolerant of other religions and refused to join in the local festivals. More seriously their refusal to do homage to the Emperor's statue left them open to the accusation of disloyalty to Caesar and the Empire.

From the time of Augustus the Roman emperors had been deified and by the time of Domitian a day was set aside each year as a religious festival recognising the divinity of the emperor. It was expected that loyal citizens, on that day, would go to the official shrine, where there would be the Emperor's statue, and take a pinch of incense to put on the altar and say the words 'Caesar is Lord'. Christians found this an impossible requirement. To say that anyone was Lord other than Messiah Jesus was blasphemy. That would have been a denial of their faith in the Lord Jesus. This day, probably the first day in August, the month named after the Emperor, became known in the Roman calendar as 'lord's day', and it was on this day that John was in the Spirit on the island of Patmos thinking of his beloved children throughout the region who would be signing their own death warrants on that day by going to the official shrine and refusing to do homage to the Emperor, but saying 'Jesus is Lord!'

The persecution of Christians continued into the reign of Trajan (AD 98 - 117) and some insight into what was happening to members of the Christian churches in the region around the Seven Churches addressed in the letters in the book of Revelation can be gained from the correspondence between the Emperor Trajan and Pliny, the Governor of Bithynia. Bithynia was the region of Asia Minor north of Galatia which Paul was forbidden by the Holy Spirit to enter. His steps were redirected to Troas where he had the vision of the 'man of Macedonia' that resulted in his crossing to the mainland of Europe.

We know that the gospel spread into the region of Bithynia in the apostolic period and there were numerous churches there to which Peter addressed his first letter (1 Peter 1:1). Pliny was faced with the problem of dealing with Christians against whom he was receiving many complaints including anonymous letters. He wrote to the Emperor for advice saying that he had examined and executed some of them but under torture the only thing he could discover about them was that they

> were wont to foregather before dawn and pledge themselves by a sacrament not to any improper behaviour, but simply to abstain from theft, immorality, and any form of dishonesty. This done, they dispersed and met later for a meal of an ordinary and harmless sort. To ascertain the truth of all this I thought fit to examine under torture two young women called deaconesses, but discovered nothing beyond a morbid fanaticism. So many people are involved that I have decided to consult you. For the mischief has spread from the towns to the countryside.

Trajan's reply was brief and to the point.

> You have followed the right course, my dear Pliny, in your examination of alleged Christians. Search must not be made; but, if accused and convicted, they must be punished – with the proviso that any who deny themselves to be Christians and prove the same by venerating our gods, should have the benefit of their recantation, whatever your suspicions of the past. Anonymous letters are not evidence; to treat them as such would be a shocking precedent, unworthy of our age.

Decline of the Roman Empire

In the final centuries of the Roman Empire the province of Asia Minor was attacked by Goths and the Temple of Artemis in Ephesus was wrecked in the year AD 262. Some sixty years later when Constantine was converted to Christianity (AD 316), many buildings became churches. Notable examples are the city finance and commerce centre in Ephesus which became the Church of the Virgin Mary; the Town Hall in Philadelphia and the Roman Baths in Hierapolis. Each of these became churches.

The Christians, however, played a part in the destruction of some of the most famous buildings from the Hellenistic period particularly attacking temples dedicated to pagan gods. Theodosius I in AD 392 encouraged this by issuing an edict closing down all the pagan shrines in the Empire. Within ten years John Chrysostom, Patriarch of Constantinople, took advantage of this edict, leading a mob to destroy the Temple of Artemis in Ephesus, seeing this as 'the final triumph of Christianity over paganism'.

The Byzantine Period

The influence of Christianity in the major cities of this region continued for nearly three hundred years following the division of the Roman Empire into East and West and the division of orthodoxy between the Roman Church and the Greek Church. The Eastern Church thrived in this region although Ephesus, Sardis and the other principal cities of the region were all sacked and ruined in AD 616 during an invasion led by the Persians.

The Seljuk Period

But it was not until the turn of the first millennium with the conquest of this area by the Seljuk dynasties with their emphasis upon the Whirling Dervishes that we see the ultimate conflict and attempt to eradicate the Greek influence. The Seljuk Sultanate was instrumental in promoting the 'Crescentades' in this region.

This is a term used to define the rapid expansion of Islam by violent means at this time. Islam spread rapidly throughout what we now know as the Middle East and even farther afield. Islamic expansion into Christian Europe and the conquest of European countries such as Spain and Islamic domination in the Holy Land led to a strong reaction of Europeans. The 'Crusades' were aimed at clearing the region of Islam and re-establishing its Christian heritage.

The Ottoman Empire

The Islamization of the region which began with the conquest of the Byzantine Empire by the Seljuks and the birth of the Ottoman Empire resulted in further neglect of historic sites and the destruction or conversion of non-Islamic religious buildings to adapt them for the use of the new religion. Many great churches all over the region were converted into mosques and Christians were either driven out or forcibly converted. Islamist policy was one of total conquest and submission of the population and enforcement of sharia, Islamic law.

Despite this policy that brought yet another period of persecution and great suffering to the Christians in the region, somehow the gospel survived. The Christian community in the region in the last quarter of the second millennium began to increase as a more relaxed form of Islam became the traditional culture. Christians and Muslims lived side-by-side for centuries until well into the twentieth century.

The Modern Period

This was the situation until the fall of the Ottoman Empire at the end of the First World War, with the conquest of the whole Middle East by the Western Allies in which the British Army played a leading role in 1919. The breaking up of the Empire led to a redistribution of the whole region regardless of ethnic groupings, and little attention was paid to groups who had lived in harmony in times past. The Allies played a major part in these political decisions, but followed a disastrous policy of hesitation and equivocation.

The war against Germany was over and there was a strong demand for the return of soldiers to civilian life. The British Army was fully stretched in overseeing the creation of the new states of Jordan, Iran and Iraq as well as undertaking responsibility for the mandate of Palestine. The French were only interested in taking control of Syria and Lebanon and had no appetite for supporting the Greek army in Anatolia against the rising power of the Turks under their new military leader Kemal who later became Kemal Ataturk, first President of the new nation of Turkey.

The Greeks made a strong appeal to London for support but most of the British government was strongly pro Turkish. Only Lloyd George the Prime Minister, and Winston Churchill were willing to help but were powerless against the rest of the Cabinet and the widespread public view that the troops should be brought home. The ancient Greek Christian community of Asia Minor that had survived the centuries was now under great threat as the Turks descended onto the coastal plain.

The great city of Smyrna that was largely Christian fell to the Turks in September 1922 and tens of thousands of Christians were slaughtered, raped and tortured. Their homes were burnt and the survivors fled. The Archbishop of Smyrna was handed over by the Turkish army to the mob to suffer mutilation and a martyr's death. The peaceful co-existence of Muslims and Christians was at an end. There were more than 1,500,000

Christians in the area who fled to the coast where a fleet of Greek vessels was mustered. British, French and Italian ships were also there to remove their nationals, and they also helped rescue many of the Greeks.

That was virtually the end of Christianity in Asia Minor after nearly 2000 years of continuous Christian presence. Turkey, from 1922, despite being declared a secular state, had no Christian churches. The ethnic cleansing of 1922 was complete. That situation except for a small Orthodox presence has been maintained through to the present day, although what will happen now that Turkey aspires to join the European Union remains to be seen. The hostility between Turkey and Greece has been maintained and can be seen in microcosm in Cyprus where the island became divided following the Turkish Army's invasion of the north in 1974.

Since the early 1990s when large scale European tourism began to develop, Turkey has been the focus of evangelistic activity from a number of 'new churches' in Britain. At the same time a number of small indigenous evangelical groups have grown in the major towns and cities. These groups have a hard time with opposition from the Muslim population and various forms of obstruction from the civil authorities.

Archaeology in the Modern Period

Over the centuries the great cities founded in the Byzantine period and earlier ages disappeared and only the abandoned ruins remained. They were largely forgotten for many centuries until the great period of European exploration which began in the nineteenth century and still continues today. Until recently there was virtually no control over archaeological expeditions from Europe and the USA and many famous relics have been transported around the world. Some of these are on show in the British Museum but the most famous is the reconstructed Altar of Zeus in Berlin.

Despite the extent of archaeological exploration during this century, vast areas of ancient cities remain undiscovered. These include sites of considerable Christian interest such as Laodicea whose ruins have until recently remained largely undisturbed since the great earthquakes of the first century AD.

Section of Entablature
at Laodicea

Since AD 2000 though, some work has been carried out by the Turkish authorities to open up Laodicea for the increasing number of Christian tourists visiting the sites of the Seven Churches. At some sites however, visitors can stroll among the remains of massive buildings where large quantities of pottery and other interesting artefacts are all around the site. So too are illegal traders offering coins and other items for sale.

Similarly at Hierapolis, at the top of the mountain overlooking Laodicea there are extensive ruins such as the old Roman Baths that became a church building. There are numerous other ruins of great buildings around Hierapolis including an extensive and highly impressive necropolis and mausoleum a short walk from the hot springs.

Chapter 2

The Early Church in the Roman Empire

The keen reader of the New Testament cannot fail to notice the difference between Paul's attitude to the Roman Empire and that expressed in the Revelation of John and in the Epistles of Peter and John. Paul, of course, wrote considerably earlier than John, but although they were all Jews, only Paul was also a Roman citizen and enjoyed all its privileges. There were many times in Paul's life when he was helped by officials of the Empire. In fact, he owed his life to their intervention on more than one occasion.

At Ephesus, when Paul was determined to go into the theatre to address the riotous mob stirred up by Demetrius, it was not only his friends, but Roman city officials who restrained him.

THE 'ICHTHUS' PAVEMENT CARVING AT EPHESUS

When a hostile mob in Jerusalem was determined to lynch him, it was members of the Roman garrison who rescued him. And when Paul was informed of the plot to assassinate him, the Romans sent a company of soldiers to guard him on the journey to Caesarea to ensure his safety.

Paul, therefore, had good reason to write to the Christians in Rome saying that all authorities were appointed by God and should be obeyed. 'For rulers hold no terror for those who do right, but for those who do wrong. Do you want to be free from fear of the one in authority? Then do what is right and he will commend you' (Romans 13:3). If Paul had been alive thirty years later when John sent the messenger from Patmos, there is no doubt he would have said something very different.

Peter, whose writings were also earlier than John's, wrote a similar instruction to the Christians in the scattered communities across Asia. He asked the rhetorical question, 'who is going to harm you if you are eager to do good?' (1 Peter 3:13). At the same time he urged the believers in Jesus not to do anything to provoke the authorities whom he said had been instituted by God. Christians were to show proper respect for everyone, to fear God and honour the Emperor. Peter referred to the painful trials and suffering that the Christians of Asia were experiencing but the context of these statements indicate insult and ridicule rather than martyrdom.

Peter wrote this letter from Rome during the reign of Nero but evidently before the violent persecution of Christians broke out following the disastrous fire that swept through the city. His words clearly indicate that although he refers to Rome as 'Babylon' he did not regard Rome as the enemy of the gospel at this point in time. In this respect Peter's experience was similar to that of Paul.

As a citizen of the Empire, Paul enjoyed all its advantages in his travels, preaching the gospel from town to town and benefiting from all the privileges of Rome's patronage. Sadly, this was a situation that did not last beyond Paul's and Peter's lifetime. Rome's attitude towards Christians changed radically in a bewilderingly short time that must have left many Christians puzzled and found others unprepared. The reasons for this rapid change are complex and they can only be understood in the context of three sets of relationships - between Jews and Rome; Jews and Christians; and Christians and Rome.

Jews and Rome

Judaism had won for itself a position of privilege within the Roman Empire. This had not been easy and had been obtained at a price. Israel had been an oppressed people for centuries before the birth of Jesus, suffering under the heel of successive empires whose armies swept through the tiny buffer state *en route* to larger conquests. The Assyrians, the Babylonians, the Egyptians, the Greeks and finally the Romans had each overrun the land of Israel and Judah.

Despite the centuries of oppression the people of Israel still held onto the promises of God that they were a covenant people whom he would use to take the knowledge of God to all nations, that his word would go out from Zion and that all peoples would see his blessings upon the tiny nation of Israel. They clung to the promises of God that the day would come when he would send Messiah to them and that in the messianic age they would enjoy the favour of God whose presence would be sought by all the nations. The prophets and priests of Israel all called for faithfulness to the teaching given to Moses and to the three distinctive features of Judaism which were - obedience to the Torah; circumcision; and observance of *Shabbat*.

With the ascendance of the Roman Empire over the whole region an accommodation was made for the religious observances of Judaism. Jews were allowed the special privilege of following their religion in return for prayers being said in the Temple and in synagogues throughout the Empire. Rome's primary concern was for peace in the regions and so long as the Jews affirmed their loyalty to the Emperor by praying for him this was sufficient to ensure that Rome would leave them in peace.

As a nation, the people of Israel had enjoyed a special position of privilege within the Empire since the days of Augustus. He treated the Jews with understanding and benevolence. He even sent regular offerings to Jerusalem for sacrifice in the Temple and asked for prayers to be said for him that God would bless him and protect him. Augustus recognized the Jews' desire to be obedient to the Torah and to observe the Sabbath. So whenever there was a distribution of food or money taking place on a Sabbath in Rome, he saved some of the distribution for the Jews to be given to them the following day, thus respecting their sacred customs.

In the earliest days after Pentecost and throughout the first ten years of the apostolic era when the gospel was being proclaimed in Jerusalem, Judea and Samaria, it was not a problem that came to the notice of Roman officials. The Apostles were Jews and their mission was to Jews. It was only when Paul and Barnabas were sent out from Antioch into the Gentile world that the gospel began to come to the notice of Roman officials.

In Cyprus, the first island evangelised by Paul, the Roman governor came to faith. Luke's record of Paul's first missionary journey says that when they left Paphos they travelled into the region of Pisidia and on the Sabbath they spoke in the synagogue in Antioch. Acts 13:15f gives a full account of Paul's sermon proclamation on that momentous day. It evidently had a dramatic impact upon his hearers who invited him to come back the following week. Luke records 'on the next Sabbath almost the whole city gathered to hear the word of the Lord. When the Jews saw the crowds, they were filled with jealousy and talked abusively against what Paul was saying' (Acts 13:44-45).

Jews and Christians

It is probably too simplistic to say that the entire motive for opposing the message brought by the Apostles was jealousy. It is useful to look at Paul's mission and message from a Jewish perspective. The leaders of the synagogue no doubt discerned that the whole future of Judaism was threatened by the message. If Jesus **was** the Messiah who had been rejected by the elders of the nation God would surely bring judgment upon the whole house of Israel. As Jews of the Dispersion they had fought hard to hold on to the traditions of their fathers. This had not been easy in an often hostile, alien environment.

They were happy to receive God-fearing Gentiles and to treat such proselytes who observed the Law of Moses as Jews, but Paul was teaching a message that undermined the whole basis of Judaism. He was telling the Gentiles, not only that they could receive the forgiveness of God through faith in Jesus but also that there was no necessity to observe the Sabbath, or to be circumcised, that these precious ordinances were now irrelevant! Paul was actually saying that these Gentile converts were **inheritors of the promises of the covenant** in exactly the same way as those who were born into the house of Israel. Outrageous! Although it is essentially in line with the message in Isaiah 56:6-7 that Jesus quoted in the temple in Jerusalem (Luke 19:46) it was more acceptable in the Diaspora than in Jerusalem.

Paul actually wrote to the **Gentile** Christians in Galatia telling them that the teaching given to Moses (the Torah) was only given to lead people to Christ and that those who put their trust in Jesus were now set free from the binding regulations of the Torah. There is no evidence that Paul extended this teaching to Jewish believers in Jesus despite the accusations of his enemies among the Judaisers. Although in Romans 3:21f Paul teaches that 'a righteousness from God, apart from the law, has been made known' and in Galatians 2:15 he declares that 'a man is not justified by observing the law, but by faith in Jesus Christ', he himself was careful to continue to live in accordance with Hebraic custom. He was totally liberated from the *obligations* of Torah observance *as a means of salvation*, but he was free to practise traditional customs if he so chose.

In fact when Paul discovered that Timothy had not been circumcised, he took steps to remedy the situation. Despite the fact that he believed all distinctions of nationality, social rank and gender have been abolished, as all are 'one in Christ' he nevertheless still practised basic observance of the law (Galatians 3: 28). This was clearly misunderstood by orthodox Jewish zealots who became haters of the gospel claiming that Paul was teaching that God had abolished the Hebrew race.

The core of the problem was that Paul taught Gentile believers that 'if you belong to Christ, then you are **Abraham's seed**, and heirs according to the promise' (Galatians 3:26-29). It is hardly surprising, therefore, that Paul was seen as a dangerous false teacher whose message threatened the very existence of Israel. He had to be stopped.

For some time Paul maintained his policy of going first to the synagogue in each city he visited. When he was rejected he went to the Gentiles. He often said that his mission was, first to the Jew and then to the Gentile. Eventually, with great sadness of heart he turned away from any mission to the Jews and saw his calling primarily as an Apostle to Gentiles. This was a costly decision as Paul's great concern for his fellow countryman is seen in the passionate declaration of Romans 9:3 that he would willingly sacrifice his own personal salvation for the sake of his brothers, the people of Israel.

The gospel enjoyed phenomenal success among the Gentiles, particularly as it was interpreted by Hellenistic Jews such as Paul,

Apollos, Priscilla, Aquila and Timothy all of whom were not only steeped in the word of God as transmitted down the centuries through Hebraic tradition but who also understood the mind of the Greeks. Timothy was typical of the new generation of Messianics. His father was Greek but both his mother and grandmother were Jews who diligently taught him the Jewish scriptures.

Everywhere the Apostles went among the Gentiles, their message came as 'good news' that was readily embraced by all classes of both men and women. By the time Paul reached Rome about the year AD 60 or 61 there were already many Gentile believers some of whom greeted him as he entered Rome (Acts 28:15). It was not long before the gospel even penetrated the ruling aristocracy. Paul was able, during his two years confinement in Rome, to say in a letter to the church in Philippi: 'All the Saints send you greetings, *especially those who belong to Caesar's household*' (Philippians 4:22).

Christians and Rome

Paul, no doubt, brought many of these Romans into the faith, but there were others who had already become Christians. Roman records show that as early as AD 57, at least three years before Paul reached Rome, Pomponia Graecina the wife of Aulus Plautius, the Roman general in charge of the conquest of Britain, was a Christian. This indicates that the gospel was actually in Britain within 25 years of Pentecost! She was sent for trial before her husband and other relations but was acquitted. It is possible that they too had some sympathy for the new teaching. Perhaps the early tradition that Joseph of Arimathea brought the gospel to Britain during the Apostolic period is true.

By AD 95 the Emperor Domitian's own niece Domitilla was a Christian and so too was her husband Flavius Clemens, the Emperor's cousin. Domitian, who by this time had become a hater of the gospel and persecutor of Christians had Flavius put to death and tried to make Domitilla marry again but finally banished her from Rome.

The success of the gospel provoked strong opposition from the Jews. In Rome, where there were both Jewish and Gentile Christians, the arguments between them were often so fierce that they caused public conflict which inevitably drew the attention of the authorities and may have been the cause for the edict of Claudius in banning Jews from Rome in AD 45. Undoubtedly the Jews blamed the Christians for their eviction and this deepened their resentment of the gospel. Priscilla and Aquila were probably banished from Rome at this time and shortly afterwards Paul met with them in Corinth, where, after considerable trouble in the synagogue, Paul finally made the decision, 'From now on I will go to the Gentiles' (Acts 18:6).

This was not only a significant day in Paul's personal life, it was a defining moment in the history of the Early Church. Luke records, 'the Jews made a united attack on Paul and brought him into court. 'This man,' they charged, 'is persuading the people to worship God in ways contrary to the law' (Acts 18:12-13). Fortunately for Paul, Gallio, the proconsul, cared nothing for Jewish Law and refused even to hear the case. When they were ejected from the court they turned on Sosthenes, the ruler of the synagogue, and publicly beat him.

The charge that Christians were breaking the laws of Rome was extremely serious and although Gallio was prepared to turn a blind eye to these public order offences, similar scenes were happening throughout the Empire wherever there were Jews of the Diaspora or Dispersion. Inevitably it came to the notice of Rome that Christians were no longer to be regarded as a Jewish sect. From this time the Christians lost the protection that had been accorded to them so long as they were under the umbrella of Judaism. They were thus exposed to the full might of Rome. Soon rumours spread that Christianity was not a harmless religious sect of Judaism but a subversive political organization refusing to acknowledge the supremacy of the Emperor and declaring itself to follow another king.

The fact that Christians refused to acknowledge the divinity of the Emperor or to attend the festivals of local pagan religions brought them charges of atheism. Moreover, Christian worship took place in private homes which further excited the curiosity of their neighbours and gave rise to false reports about their secret activities. Rumours spread that the Christians were involved in child murder, that at the Eucharist they ate the flesh and drank the blood of humans. Soon they were regarded as the enemies of mankind and there were many people in every community who were happy to denounce them to the authorities. The way was paved for the terrible persecutions that marred the first two centuries of the church.

Nero was the first Emperor to mount a full-scale attack upon the Christians but his motive was not religious but more one of self-survival. The aristocracy of Rome hated the vulgar antics of the Emperor who was hugely popular with the common people and depended upon the mob for maintaining his power. When the disastrous fire of July AD 64 swept through Rome causing thousands of people to be homeless, rumours abounded that Nero himself had started the fire. It was in the face of these charges of arson that Nero had to find a scapegoat. He found one in the Christians who were already unpopular in the city and since they did not practise circumcision or keep *Shabbat* they were now seen as separated from Judaism and therefore no longer open to the protection of Rome.

The charge that Nero started the fire is well-documented by Roman writers such as Pliny, Suetonius and Tacitus. The latter gives a famous account that is important for an understanding of the beginnings of the persecution of Christians in the Roman Empire that lasted for nearly 200 years. Tacitus writes:

> To get rid of the rumour, Nero put in his own place as culprits, and subjected to the most refined punishments, the men whom the common people hated for their secret crimes, and called Christians. Christ, from whom they had that name, had been put to death in the reign of Tiberius by the procurator, Pontius Pilate, and the pernicious superstition was checked for a while. Afterwards it began to break out afresh, not only in Judea, where the mischief had arisen, but in Rome also, where all sorts of murder and filthy shame from all quarters met together and became the fashion.
>
> In the first place some were seized and made to confess, then on their information, a vast multitude was convicted on charges not so much of arson as of hatred for the human race. They were not only put to death, but put to death with insult, in that they were dressed up in the skins of beasts to perish either by the worrying of dogs or on crosses, or by fire, or when the daylight failed, they were burnt to serve as lights by night.
>
> Nero had thrown open his gardens for that spectacle, and was giving a circus performance, joining the rabble in a jockey's dress, or driving a chariot. Hence, compassion arose, though it was for men who were criminals and deserved the severest penalties, on the grounds that they were not destroyed for the good of the state, but to satisfy the cruelty of an individual. *(Tacitus Annals XV 44.5)*

Tacitus distinguished two stages in the proceedings. First, individuals were charged with arson and a few confessions were obtained by torture. This led to many arrests, but now the charge was changed to that of 'hatred of the human race'. By this, Tacitus meant that the Christians were regarded as disloyal to the Empire and unconcerned about society in general. The evidence for this was said to be found in their secret rituals as they met in their home groups. This was a highly significant change of emphasis that opened the way for Christians throughout the Empire to be regarded as criminals.

By the time Domitian came to the throne the mere admission of membership of a Christian group was sufficient for someone to be regarded as guilty and deserving of punishment. This is made clear in the correspondence between Pliny and the Emperor Trajan (AD 98 – AD 110) quoted in Chapter One in which Trajan affirmed that any self-confessed Christian should be punished but he also warned that there should not be any deliberate searching for Christians and that anonymous accusations should be ignored as being inconsistent with the values of the age..

Both Peter and Paul are thought to have lost their lives in Rome at the time of Nero's purge of the Church. Clement, the Bishop of Rome, writing about 30 years later, in AD 96, said that Peter was crucified and Paul, as a Roman citizen, was beheaded. The dates for their deaths would therefore have been somewhere between July 64 and the end of AD 66. It is an intriguing question as to what Paul did between his acquittal in Rome in AD 62 or 63 and his death!

Despite the murder of the two most prominent Apostles this was not the end of the Apostolic era of mission. The persecution of believers had begun in Jerusalem within a few years of Pentecost and was sparked by the stoning of Stephen. The Orthodox Jews of Jerusalem were outraged by the preaching of this Hellenist who had the temerity to accuse them of betraying and murdering the Messiah and of failing to obey the Law of Moses (Acts 7:52-53).

The Jerusalem Church

Very little is known of the history of the Jerusalem Church other than what is contained in the Acts of the Apostles and occasional references in the Pauline Epistles. The strategy of mission given by Jesus in Acts 1:8 to take the gospel to the whole world, going from

Jerusalem, through Judea, then Samaria and finally to the Gentile nations was certainly followed by the Apostles and their disciples. We read of Peter and John being sent from Jerusalem to investigate what was happening in Samaria through the preaching of Philip and that they themselves had a share in this mission. 'Peter and John returned to Jerusalem, preaching the gospel in many Samaritan villages' (Acts 8:25).

We know also that the Apostles were still in Jerusalem at the time of the Council of Jerusalem around AD 49 - 50. This was called to settle the problems arising from the conversion of Gentiles. And James, as the nearest blood relative of Jesus was the presiding Elder. Although he himself lived as an orthodox Jew he evidently fully concurred with the decision of the Council which seemed 'good to the Holy Spirit' and all those present. In a letter to the churches signed by James the decision was given not to burden the Gentiles with anything beyond that of abstaining from food sacrificed to idols, from involvement in pagan festivals, and sexual immorality. But the prohibition upon attending pagan festivals led to the separation of Christians from social events in the local communities which led directly to persecution.

For the next 14 years the New Testament is largely silent about events in Jerusalem, although there are accounts in other literature of the life of James who was known as 'James the Just' and was said to have been regarded as a holy man even by opponents of the gospel. His murder in AD 64 at the instigation of Zealots among the Sadducees is said to have shocked the Pharisees who blamed the murderers for bringing judgment upon the city in the following years.

Roman rule in Judea and the Galilee at this time was reflecting the chaos that reigned in Nero's Rome and this lack of organization and firm government encouraged the Zealots in Jerusalem. In AD 66 a full-scale revolt broke out with the massacre of the Roman garrison in the city. Vespasian was the general in charge of the legions in that part of the Empire. He first of all subdued Galilee and was about to advance on Jerusalem when the army proclaimed him Emperor and he departed for Rome. His son Titus took over command of the legions and laid siege to Jerusalem. The suffering inside the city was intense and when at last the Romans broke through and slaughtered the survivors, destroying the temple and much of the city, it was virtually the end of the Jewish state. The last Zealots held out in the stronghold of Masada, but when the Roman ramp neared the top of the walls of the fortress they committed mass suicide. In vain they had waited for God to intervene and send his long expected Messiah tragically not realising that he had already come and been rejected by the elders of the nation.

When Jerusalem fell in AD 70 there were no Christians left in the city. The Christians had received a prophecy ahead of the revolt in AD 66 reminding them of the prophetic words of Jesus, 'When you see Jerusalem being surrounded by armies, you will know that its desolation is near. Then let those who are in Judea flee to the mountains, let those in the city get out, and let those in the country not go into the city' (Luke 21:20-21). Most of the Christians in Judea fled across the Jordan to Pella, but others went west into Asia Minor that was rapidly becoming the most populous area for Christian churches. Among them, tradition asserts, were the Apostle John and Mary the mother of Jesus.

The Expanding Gentile Church

According to Irenaeus, John was banished by the Romans to Patmos, but after the death of Domitian and during the short reign of Nerva, John was released and continued in active ministry from Ephesus, visiting and encouraging the churches in the region and planting new fellowships. He must have been quite elderly then so the tradition that John died in Ephesus at the end of the first century and was buried there is well founded.

It is highly significant for our understanding of the growth of the church in the first two centuries beyond Pentecost to note that after the death of Paul there was no great missionary travelling across the Empire for 100 years yet the church grew at a phenomenal rate. Pliny notes in his correspondence with Trajan that followers of Jesus were to be found in large numbers not only in the cities but also in the countryside. He also says that attendance at pagan festivals of the local gods had dropped significantly.

This is evidence for the unique appeal of the gospel to all classes of men and women. It demonstrates that evangelism was not dependent upon the Apostles or upon the work of itinerant preachers. Church growth in the first and second centuries occurred through the natural processes of believers living a lifestyle that was different from the rest of the population and was sufficiently attractive to make friends and neighbours want to know more about the faith. Of course, it also excited opponents whose opposition sometimes led to mob violence.

But the way in which Christians died was an even more powerful witness than the way in which they lived.

When Ignatius the Bishop of Antioch in Pisidia was condemned to death he was taken on foot, making the long journey overland to Rome. At each town or city that he passed through the Christian community gathered around him to greet him and to listen to his witness and teaching. Ignatius had been brought to the Lord by John and was the last remaining link with the Apostles so his testimony was of great importance to the Church. On the long journey he wrote seven letters that have been preserved and form a very important source of information about the organization and life of the Early Church.

In every place where Ignatius met with believers he urged them not to try to save his life and in a similar vein, from Smyrna, he wrote to the Church in Rome pleading with them not to try to save him. His death in Rome underlined Tertullian's assessment of the significance of martyrdom in the spread of the gospel in his well-known words, 'the blood of the martyrs is the seed of the Church.'

Chapter 3

Biblical Context

At the time of the crucifixion Jesus entrusted his mother into the care of John, the brother of James, probably the youngest of the disciples. Sometime later, probably soon after the scattering of the believers from Jerusalem following the martyrdom of Stephen, John took Mary and left Judea. According to tradition, they travelled to Asia Minor and settled in Ephesus.

The Apostolic Ministry in Asia Minor

We know much more about Paul's ministry in Ephesus than we do about John's, although John probably lived there for more than fifty years, whereas Paul only stayed for three years. There is no record of Paul and John meeting during Paul's ministry in the province, which has led some scholars to believe that John arrived after Paul's departure. This would place John and Mary's arrival after AD 45 which would mean that Mary must have been about sixty-five years of age, perhaps somewhat elderly to make the hazardous journey from Jerusalem. The reason for the silence of the New Testament on John's ministry in Ephesus may simply be that the contact with John and Mary was of no great interest to Luke in his record of Paul's ministry.

John had an intimate knowledge of the churches around the Roman province of Asia. There must certainly have been some overlap of John's and Paul's ministry because we know that Paul visited some of the places addressed in the Seven Churches. The little group of churches at Colossae, Laodicea and Hierapolis were all on Paul's itinerary although Paul acknowledges that it was Epaphras who planted the church at Colossae. All three churches are mentioned in the greetings in Colossians 4:13-16

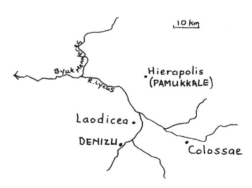

where Paul also speaks of a letter he had written to the Laodiceans which, sadly, has been lost. According to tradition, John continued preaching the gospel in the province of Asia from his base in Ephesus long after Paul's final departure from the area.

Paul in Ephesus

Acts 20:13f records that Paul did not visit Ephesus on his final travels through the area because he was in a hurry to reach Jerusalem in time for Pentecost. Instead he sailed into Miletus via Samos and from Miletus he sent across the bay for the Elders of the church at Ephesus so that he could give them his farewell greetings and exhortations. It may be that Paul did not wish to visit Ephesus due to the uproar created by the silversmiths shortly before he had left the city. He may not have wished to be seen again and to face delays in travelling to Jerusalem if there were further protests at his presence. The church at Ephesus is the first of the Seven Churches addressed in the Book of Revelation. Ephesus was the most important city for the gospel in the province of Asia and there were a number of well-known names associated with the church there: Paul, Aquila and Priscilla, Apollos, Gaius, Erastus, Onesiphorus, Timothy and John.

Ephesus had strong connections with Paul although it is doubtful if Paul actually founded the church there, since on his arrival for his second visit the believers said that they had not even heard of the Holy Spirit (Acts 19:2) which Paul would surely have included in his teaching. Paul had earlier made a short visit together with Priscilla and Aquila who stayed in Ephesus. Paul himself had spoken in the synagogue and had clearly been well received because he was asked to stay and spend more time explaining his message. He declined but promised to return.

On his second visit he stayed between two and a half and three years, the longest he spent in any one place, teaching first in the synagogue for three months but then after being rejected by the Jews, continuing in a rented hall with an increasingly Gentile congregation and also teaching from house to house. Acts 19:9 says that Paul ceased speaking in the synagogue and transferred his teaching to the hall of Tyrannus. The 'Western text' adds the words 'between the hours of 11am and 4 pm'. This has been seen by some scholars as evidence that Paul concentrated his mission upon the lower working classes and slaves who would have been the only ones likely to have attended his lectures during these siesta hours.

It is, however, highly unlikely that the main direction of Paul's mission was to the urban poor. Rather, this is evidence that the gospel had **universal** appeal. There is plenty of evidence of the conversion of men and women of high social rank, men like Erastus who was the City Treasurer. At the height of the riot in Ephesus led by the silversmiths, who made images of the goddess Artemis, Paul wanted to go into the theatre and address the crowd but he was prevented from so doing by a number of high-ranking officials in the city who were evidently either believers or sympathetic to Paul's mission.

The Church at Ephesus

Paul left Timothy in charge of the fellowship after the riot made him decide that it was time to leave the city. Timothy was probably replaced by the Apostle John who, according to tradition, pastored the church at Ephesus until the end of the century. Paul's letters to Timothy were sent to Ephesus and it is generally thought that 1 John was also addressed to Ephesus.

Some scholars query whether 'Ephesians' was written exclusively to the city of Ephesus or was a more general letter to Gentile believers in the region and addressed to Ephesus because of its importance as the capital city of the province, raised to that status by the Emperor Augustus. It is somewhat strange that in view of the length of time Paul spent in Ephesus there are no personal references to the situation there as, for example, in Corinth, and there are statements such as 'ever since I heard about your faith' (1:13) and 'surely you have heard about God's grace that was given to me' (3:2). These comments do not indicate an intimate knowledge of the Christians in Ephesus where Paul had spent longer than anywhere else on his travels.

Despite these difficulties there is plenty of information in the record in Acts about the church in Ephesus. In his final words to the elders who came to Miletus to bid him farewell when he was on the way to Jerusalem before going to Rome, Paul prophesied that savage wolves would come among the people. It would appear from the letter addressed to that city in Revelation 2 that this is exactly what did happen in Ephesus. They became the target of itinerant preachers bringing a variety of different teachings. The letter indicates that the believers had held fast to the authentic gospel originally brought to them but that in the process they had lost their first love.

The Nicolaitans were the prime target of criticism in the letter, but not very much is known about them. They were clearly a sect whose teaching and practices were heretical. Both Irenaeus and Hippolytus say that the leader of this sect was Nicolas who was originally one of the Seven Deacons named in Acts 6:5 and who fell away from the faith. The teaching of the Nicolaitans was more philosophical than theological. They said that there was no connection between body and soul. This meant that anything that happened to the body did not affect the spiritual state of the soul and thus opened the way for personal physical indulgence, leading to obesity or sexual immorality, or both.

John speaks about some members of the fellowship falling away and warns the believers to test every spirit because of the false prophets who had gone out into the world. He questions whether they were ever true believers. He says 'They went out from us, but they did not really belong to us. For if they had belonged to us, they would have remained with us; but their going out showed that none of them belonged to us' (1 John 2:19 & 4:1).

The twin themes of love and unity feature strongly in Paul's letter to the Ephesians. Paul was deeply concerned to emphasise the oneness in Christ, of Jew and Gentile, and to urge the believers to love one another and to 'live a life of love, just as Christ loved us' (Ephesians 5:2). His warnings about immorality would also have been very apposite for those who lived in Ephesus (5:5) due to the widespread practices of sexual perversions linked with the fertility cult of the goddess Artemis that included homosexual excesses of various kinds. The evidence of this is still to be seen in the ruins of Ephesus today.

Apostolic Teaching

Throughout his lifetime Paul personally kept to orthodox Jewish practices and even in a solidly Roman Gentile city such as Philippi, where there was no synagogue, he observed Shabbat by going out to a place of prayer beside the river, outside the city gate (Acts 16:13). There is, however, a reference to Paul breaking bread on the first day of the week but he had just been observing Passover at Philippi (or Neapolis which served as the port for Philippi - see Acts 20:6). Bringing the people together in Troas on the evening of the first day of the week may simply have been because he was leaving the next day and was hoping to reach Jerusalem in time for Pentecost (Acts 20:7).

We do not know how long John continued ministering in the area before his arrest and banishment to the island of Patmos. Neither do we know the circumstances of his arrest although clearly from his own testimony it was because he was preaching the gospel of Jesus. We can, however, be fairly confident of the date of John's receiving the Revelation as being between the years AD 94 and 96, the time of the Domitian persecution.

The Message given to John

In Revelation 1:9-11 John sets the scene describing how he was on the island of Patmos when he was caught up in the Holy Spirit and received the revelation that he was instructed to write on a scroll and send to seven churches 'to Ephesus, Smyrna, Pergamum, Thyatira, Sardis, Philadelphia and Laodicea'. The particular day, as already noted in Chapter 1, is highly significant. In most English translations it is 'the Lord's Day' and this is spelt with a capital L and capital D indicating that it was on the first day of the week. But the practice of observing the first day of the week as a distinctively holy day for worship was not widespread at that time. Throughout the apostolic era, the church which included a significant number of Messianics, even in Gentile areas, was still largely observant of Judaic practices.

The reference in Revelation 1:10 to 'the lord's day' was an opportunity for citizens in the provinces to reaffirm their loyalty to Rome. Rome did not mind how many gods anyone worshipped so long as its citizens paid deference to the Emperor. To Christians this was no longer just a matter of showing respect to those in authority because of the divinity accorded to Augustus. They were faced with a conflict of allegiance – the Lordship of the Emperor or the Lordship of Christ.

In Pergamum, Antipas had already been put to death for his fortitude in declaring the Lordship of Jesus and being a faithful witness even to death. John knew that many others would be following the same path, as the persecution under Domitian gathered momentum. The pages of church history would be written in the blood of the martyrs. For John, who had probably planted some of these churches and knew both the leaders and people, it was an agonising experience to be separated from them on the island of Patmos from where he could look across the sea towards Miletus and his beloved Ephesus. The message given to him by the Lord Jesus was startling in its urgency, frightening in its revelation of things to come, and yet encouraging and faith-building in its assurance of final victory.

Message and Messenger

The instruction to John was to write the message on a scroll and to send it to all the Seven Churches. The seven lampstands and the seven stars refer to the churches and the messengers. There may have been more than one church in each place – but they were each addressed as one. This meant sending a messenger on the long trek around these seven churches and staying in each place, not simply to read the message to that church but to read the whole scroll so that each church would know the message to the others as well as to their own situation and each church would receive the whole Revelation given to John from the beginning to the final 'Amen' and *Maranatha* 'come Lord Jesus'.

It is very probable that the messenger would have stayed long enough in each fellowship for the scroll to be copied so that each church possessed its own copy and the messenger would have been able to give news of John and to discuss with the elders in each place the implications of the message. Leaders from other churches in the region would no doubt also come to each of the Seven to receive the message. The reference *'he who has an ear to hear let him hear what the Spirit is saying to the churches'* is in the plural and is intended to include fellowships in the area around each of the cities to which the messenger was sent.

In Revelation 1:12-18 John attempts to describe the one who spoke to him who he says was 'like a son of man'. The numerous metaphors he uses are all symbols of authority, parts of which are used in the opening salutation of the message to each of the churches. These references are particularly relevant to the situation in that church. Hence to Ephesus the words are 'to him who holds the seven stars in his right hand'; to Smyrna they are the words of 'him who is the first and the last' (the alpha and omega) and to Pergamum they are the words of him 'who has the sharp, double-edged sword'. The significance of these will be noted later.

Format of the Message

The format of each letter follows roughly the same course although the messages vary according to local circumstances. The basic format is:

1. opening salutation
2. a brief description of the situation in the local church with commendations and words of encouragement to the believers
3. the things that are not pleasing to God
4. a promise to the overcomers.

The word 'overcomer' is common to all seven messages and the warnings and exhortations are all directed towards this end. Despite whatever may happen in the coming days, if the believers held tightly to faith in the Lord Jesus they would be overcomers. Although the promise in each place is different they are all assurances of eternal life and blessing. None of the churches is shown to be perfect but all are exhorted to greater faithfulness.

Theme and Date of the Message

A major theme of all seven letters is that of persecution. John's purpose appears to be that of strengthening believers so that they would be able to withstand the horrors of physical torture and death without denying their faith in the Lord Jesus. John evidently had had a long ministry in the area and probably would have known personally all the churches in the region as Ephesus was a major centre of communication, one of the arteries of the Empire. Even if he did not travel much in his old age John would have received visitors from the hundreds of churches scattered across the province so that he would have had an intimate knowledge of the progress of the Christian mission and the health of the fellowships.

We do not know why John was banished to the island of Patmos but it is possible to date the revelation that he received there as being during the persecution of Domitian which lasted two years from AD 94 to 96. Antipas had already been martyred in Pergamum so it is likely that the letters were written in the middle of that period, that is, AD 95.

Purpose and Relevance of the Message

The message to the Seven Churches adds significantly to the understanding of the letters in the New Testament as well as to events in the Acts of the Apostles. They help these early churches to come alive for us in the twenty-first century as they were written towards the end of the first century and tell us about the progress and growth of the church at the end of the apostolic age. They have relevance for the church today where Christians in many places are living in similar crisis times to those depicted here.

For those who study the New Testament there is added interest in the area around Laodicea as we know that it was visited by Paul on his missionary journeys in the region. We know also that Paul wrote a letter to the church in Laodicea that has been lost (Colossians 4:16). Paul's final greetings in the letter to the Colossians give some interesting insights into the activity of the early Christians in this area. There was constant communication between the three main churches of Hierapolis, Laodicea and Colossae, all three of which may have been planted by Epaphras of whom Paul speaks of as 'one of you' (Colossians 4:12).

It is not difficult to imagine the emotional stress being experienced by the Apostle John, exiled from the mainland and separated from his beloved people at the very time when they needed him most. He longed to give pastoral counselling and to embrace with the love of Christ those whom he had brought to faith in the Lord Jesus. The vision he was given on that awesome day was to enable him to write a message to the churches he knew so well and to send that message right across the hundreds of churches in the region who were suffering at the hands of their persecutors, or being betrayed by friends and neighbours and any who wished to curry favour with the authorities.

The message of the book of Revelation was given in such a way that if it fell into the hands of those who were hostile to the gospel it would not be understood. It is full of references to both the Christian Scriptures and the Hebrew Scriptures although there are no direct quotes. Those who read the messages on the scroll would have to know their Scriptures in order to understand the message. It was written in code that would only have been understood by the believers and even among them it may well have required interpretation, first by the messenger to whom John had entrusted the precious scroll to take around to the Seven Churches, and then by the elders of fellowships among whom the message was read.

The messenger would have spent some time in each city with the believers, reading not just the message to that church, or the messages to all Seven Churches but the **whole** book of Revelation. The scroll would no doubt have been copied and copies kept by the fellowship before the messenger departed on the next stage of his journey. In this way the message would have been spread widely across the region served by the Seven Churches.

The primary purpose of the messages to the churches was to assure them of the love of the Lord Jesus for them in the time of their trial; to strengthen their faith; to encourage them and to pinpoint any weaknesses in the fellowship, calling them to repentance so that the Lord could strengthen them with the power of the Holy Spirit as the days of persecution intensified.

The messages were intended to show that those who stood firm in their faith, withstanding the temptations that were all around them in a pagan, hostile environment, would be rewarded. Those who were faithful even to death through their loyalty to Jesus were thereby assured of a place in Paradise. Their names would be written in the 'Book of Life' and would never be blotted out.

Both those who withstood temptation and those who were martyred for their faith were 'the overcomers'. They were following in the footsteps of Jesus who was the archetypal 'Overcomer'. He had not only conquered temptation but had also conquered death. He was the firstborn in the kingdom of God and those who followed him were certain to be with him in the place where he had gone to be with his Father.

The overcomers were the conquerors referred to by Paul in Romans 8:37:

> In all these things we are more than conquerors through him who loved us. For I am convinced that neither death nor life, neither angels nor demons, neither the present nor the future, nor any powers, neither height nor depth, nor anything else in all creation, will be able to separate us from the love of God that is in Christ Jesus our Lord.

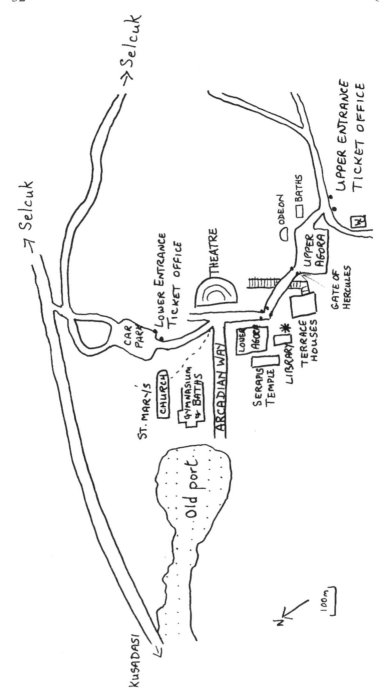

EPHESUS SKETCH MAP
(* shows the site of the Hall of Tyrannus)

Part 2   The Seven Churches

Chapter 4

Message to the Church in Ephesus

What the Visitor Sees Today

Location

Ephesus is no longer a coastal town as it was in Paul's and John's day. They would have seen a thriving port city on the north bank of the mouth of the River Cayster with the coastal town of Miletus in the next bay. If the apostles had wanted to travel from Ephesus to Miletus they would have had to take a boat. Today it is a coach ride through the cotton fields.

The ancient site of Ephesus today lies some four miles back from the Aegean Sea, south of the modern city of Selcuk, and is probably the best preserved of all of the ancient sites within the region. No-one lives there. This is mainly a result of the silting up of the River Cayster. During Alexander the Great's time the city's harbour was dredged of silt to keep the great port open and work began on re-siting a new Ephesus on the top of Ayasoluk hill between Mount Pion and Mount Koressos. It was a losing battle against nature and during the reign of the Emperor Justinian 527–564 silting turned the whole valley into a malaria-infested swamp causing the city finally to be abandoned.

Once its commercial lifeline with the sea had been severed, the fate of the great city of Ephesus was sealed. This, in part, accounts for the survival of many of the spectacular buildings in Graeco / Roman Ephesus which although shaken and damaged by devastating earthquakes such as the great quake of AD 17 were never destroyed by enemy armies. But the new site of the city of Ephesus on the top of the hill **was** sacked in AD 616 in an invasion by the Sassenids and later fell to the Turks in 1090. The modern town of Selcuk has been built at the foot of the hill nearer to the sea.

Walking through the City

Most tours of ancient Ephesus begin at the top of the hill leaving visitors to walk down the main street to rejoin their coaches at the bottom.

When leaving the coaches at the top visitors are surrounded by traders offering a variety of guidebooks and souvenirs. Upon entering the city gates visitors are able to gain some insight into the experience of first century travellers and to know the procedure that would have confronted Paul and Timothy, John and Mary and other Christian evangelists who entered the city.

Ephesus was a well-organised and efficiently regulated city with strict immigration procedures designed to protect the health and well-being of its citizens. All caravans, chariots and other means of transport had to be left outside the city gates just as the coaches and taxis are today.

The first building inside the gates was the baths. All visitors were required to wash their bodies on entering the city. Next they had to go into the city hall where the rules of the city were displayed on the walls and columns. These had to be read and studied. It was noted that some effort needed to be made to read them as some were rather high up! The visitor then went into a small theatre where they were addressed by the city elders who elaborated the rules and regulations of the city. This ensured that everyone was familiar with the customs of the city and the norms of behaviour that would be expected. All these areas can be seen today around the uppermost entrance.

The Christian visitor sees the spiritual significance of this in terms of entering the Kingdom. As new converts we first have to leave behind the baggage of the world. We are then washed of the sins of the world through baptism after which we receive the Word of God which is expounded by the elders. Finally we are free to enjoy living in the City of God.

The route through Ephesus is usually crowded with tourists at all times of the year which gives it a bustling cosmopolitan atmosphere somewhat similar to the crowded city streets in Paul's and John's day. By the second century its population is reported to have grown to around 400,000 so the main streets would probably have been as crowded as they are today.

Parts of Ephesus have been extensively excavated and many of its public buildings, particularly along the main street called the Marble Way and Curetes Street, have been restored to resemble their appearance in the first and second centuries AD. Some of this restoration is clearly not of a very high standard but as nobody lives here any more it serves to enable the visitor to get a clearer picture of part of the ancient city.

About half way down on the left hand, you will see the remains of the Temple of Domitian, who was the tyrannical emperor when John was writing his vision. He referred to himself as 'Ruler and God' and his temple was erected at great expense on the best and most central site in the town. The temple contained a colossal statue of Domitian, of which the head and forearm are in the Izmir museum. It is estimated that in a sitting position, the statue would have been five metres high and standing it would have measured seven metres (E Akurgal). Perhaps John and the believers in the churches rejoiced at John's vision of the all-powerful Jesus in Revelation 1, in contrast to the huge statue of the emperor.

Some restoration work in this area is still in progress on private homes. This is revealing central heating systems, en-suite bedrooms and elaborate marble mosaic floors. These run alongside the main street on the way down towards the magnificent Celsus Library.

THE CELSUS LIBRARY AT EPHESUS

(the site of Tyrannus' hall where Paul lectured is just to the left of this)

On the main street running downhill from the Odeon at the top to the Library below are numerous public buildings of interest such as would have been found in many cities of this period – two spacious agoras (market places), four temples, three gymnasia (schools or universities), three public toilets (where the users sat side by side probably exchanging local gossip), an odeon concert hall, a library and theatres of various sizes. The well-preserved public toilets, sitting round in a square, always excite the interest of visitors. Some of the larger buildings were constructed as monuments glorifying successive Roman Emperors.

The Christian visitor should look for signs on the pavement showing the presence of Christian believers from the early church period. These consist of the 'Ichthus' sign, or sign of the fish, in a form which later became the Maltese Cross. (The Greek word for 'fish' é÷èõò, represented the Greek initials of the words Jesus, Christ, God, Son, Saviour or Jesus Christ, Son of God  our Saviour). In troubled times when a Christian met a stranger he would sometimes make the Ichthus sign in the dust on the ground to see if the stranger recognised it and responded accordingly.

In the tourist-crowded High Street the account of the riot at Ephesus (Acts 19) during Paul's ministry comes to life. It is not difficult to imagine Demetrius, leader of the Silversmith's Trade Union, leading a noisy crowd of workers, swelled by many other citizens, down towards the Library and on to the great theatre, the largest in Asia Minor. The riotous mob filled the 24,000 seat theatre chanting 'Great is Artemis of the Ephesians!'. They maintained this chant for some two hours, the sound of which must have reverberated across the whole valley.

This theatre was the traditional focal point of the Midsummer Festival Birthday celebrations of the fertility goddess Artemis when her statue was paraded through the city streets before being returned to its Temple. The well-restored theatre is largely as it was in Paul's day. Standing down in the area of the proscenium looking up at the vast array of seats, gives some idea of the bravery of Paul who wanted to go in to address the howling crowd who had already seized two of his companions - Gaius and Aristarchus (Acts 19:23 - 41). Even just standing there today is an awesome experience and it brings to life the scene when Paul's friends struggled to dissuade him from entering the theatre; an action which would almost certainly have provoked the mob to violence from which Paul might not have escaped with his life.

Beyond the great theatre the road bears sharp right towards the gate leading out to the car park where the coaches await the tour parties; there is a small footpath on the left hand side leading down towards the ancient harbour with its second century Roman Baths. Here may also be found the ruins of the Church of St Mary the Virgin. Most Turkish guides are unaware of its existence so the Christian visitor has to know where to look for a very significant piece of early church history. The basic chancel of the church is well preserved and is a lovely place to sit and pray in the open air. The building was originally built by the Romans early in the second century when Ephesus was the banking centre for the region. It served as the city Financial Exchange but was taken over for Christian worship soon after the conversion of Constantine in AD 316.

It became the most important church of the region and was renowned throughout the Empire. The church in Ephesus was evidently already of considerable strength and status by the fifth century as it was in this building that the important Council of Ephesus took place in AD 431. This was one of the great Councils of the early church that were called to settle questions of doctrine and to establish orthodox belief and practice including the canon of Scripture. It was at the first Council of Ephesus that two great heresies were confronted, those of Pelagius and Nestorius and also where it was accepted as dogma that Jesus, the son of the Virgin Mary was also the Son of God – he was both **fully** human and **fully** divine.

If you walk down the grassy roofless nave of the church of St Mary the Virgin and turn right into a side transept there is what is probably the oldest remaining baptistry in the world with steps down either side into a central pool. It provides evidence that believers' baptism by total immersion was the practice in the Early Church. Just to the south of the church there is a vast unexcavated area of the city believed to have been a gymnasium and baths complex with many other public buildings not yet identified.

NIKE, GODDESS OF VICTORY

(This relief can be seen on Curetes Street near the Temple of Domitian - p.34)

Outside the City

The Temple of Artemis (Diana) is some 1200 metres away from ancient Ephesus towards Selcuk. The earliest traces of its foundations date back to the seventh century BC with a major restoration taking place in the following century under the Lydian King Croesus and again in 356 BC. This was the original site of the Temple to Cybele who was assimilated into the Greek pantheon by linking her worship with the goddess Artemis, twin sister of Apollo and revered as the virgin goddess of nature and protectress of women in childbirth.

Both Artemis and Apollo were the children of Zeus considered to be the father of all gods. The Temple of Artemis was destroyed and rebuilt a number of times, but its impressive ruins give some indication of the popularity of this fertility goddess in the time when Christianity first appeared on the scene. When the Temple was destroyed in 353 BC on Alexander's birthday, he promised to build not only a temple but also a new city. The Hellenistic Artemisium erected on the pattern of the archaic Artemisium in the mid fourth century BC was listed as one of the Seven Wonders of the Ancient World. It was destroyed in a raid by Goths in the third century and finally destroyed by Christians in AD 401. Today this once great city of pagan worship has only one of its impressive columns left standing.

A short coach ride away, on the slopes of Ayasoluk, the Emperor Justinian, during the sixth century, replaced an earlier wooden basilica over the traditional site of the **Grave of St John** with a magnificent basilica and dedicated it to the Apostle. During the seventh and eighth centuries when Ephesus was under constant siege from the Arabs a great wall was built from stones taken from the Gymnasium on the ancient site which helped to fortify the church.

Close by is the **Ephesus Museum** constructed in 1964 and enlarged to seven different halls in 1979. This contains the more recently excavated findings from this site as prior to the Second World War any artefacts of value were transported to Vienna and farther afield. Although there are still many historic findings from all the civilisations that once occupied Ephesus displayed in other countries, this museum is growing rapidly.

Modern Selcuk and the **Home of Mary** are often included in the itinerary for Christians due to the tradition that Mary the Mother of Jesus spent her last days here being cared for by John. Some Catholic sisters in the nineteenth century had a vision of the site of her home which is now a tourist attraction.

First Century Ephesus

Background

Ephesus, together with Antioch of Syria and Alexandria of Egypt, was one of the three great cities of the Eastern Mediterranean and when Paul spent nearly three years there it would have been bustling with life from the docks at the lower end, through the commercial and residential areas, to the Acropolis at the top of the hill. At the end of the first century when this letter was written to the church there, it had a population of some 300,000 people.

Its origins on this site date back to 1400 or 1300 BC and for most of that time it would have been known as an important centre of trade and commerce. In antiquity the City of Ephesus was located on several different sites. Most archaeologists agree that the present site excavated is the fifth.

Ephesus would have been well known to Mark Anthony and Cleopatra who were defeated in a sea battle with Octavianus (Octavius) in 31 BC. Octavianus followed them to Egypt and, on the outskirts of Alexandria, Anthony took his own life after hearing a false report that Cleopatra was dead. On hearing this she also committed suicide leaving Octavianus master of the whole Roman Empire. Octavianus took the name Caesar Augustus and declared Ephesus to be the capital of the province of Asia instead of Pergamum. This secured Ephesus as the most important religious, economic and cultural city in the region and it became a magnet for the rich and fashionable

There is very little to add to the description of Ephesus in the above section. It is the best preserved and most heavily restored of all the sites of the Seven Churches, therefore what is to be seen today is largely representative of what it would have looked like in the first century at the time of Paul's visit and the ministry of John.

As the main centre for the worship of Artemis, the fertility nature goddess, and for the production of images of her made by the local craftsmen, it is inevitable that there would have been considerable evidence of sexual practices and perversions. Archaeologists have recently discovered an underground tunnel running from the library to the brothel across the street and many obscene carved stone images have been discovered. It was against this background that Paul began his ministry in the city.

Paul was surrounded also by a great deal of demonic activity that he confronted in his usual forthright manner with such success that others tried to imitate him, calling upon the name of Jesus and commanding evil spirits to leave the possessed. This produced disastrous results for the imitators, although it enhanced Paul's reputation and considerably advanced the gospel in the region (Acts 19:11-20).

As a busy sea port as well as a centre of commerce and communications, being on one of the main arteries of the Empire, Ephesus would have had many visitors as well as sailors and was a renowned city of vice. Nevertheless, the church grew rapidly in the city and the surrounding area as Luke records in Acts 19:20 where he describes the success of Paul's ministry in converting those who practised sorcery. He says 'in this way the word of the Lord spread widely and grew in power'.

The Biblical Text (Revelation 2:1-7)

To the angel of the church in Ephesus write:

These are the words of him who holds the seven stars in his right hand and walks among the seven golden lampstands. I know your deeds, your hard work and your perseverance. I know that you cannot tolerate wicked men, that you have tested those who claim to be apostles but are not, and have found them false. You have persevered and endured hardships for my name, and have not grown weary.

Yet I hold this against you: You have forsaken your first love. Remember the height from which you have fallen! Repent and do the things you did at first. If you do not repent, I will come to you and remove your lampstand from its place. But you have this in your favour: You hate the practices of the Nicolaitans, which I also hate.

He who has an ear let him hear what the Spirit says to the churches. To him who overcomes, I will give the right to eat from the tree of life, which is in the paradise of God.

What the Ephesian Christians would have heard

Opening salutation

In the first of the seven messages, the opening declaration would have set the scene for all the messages. 'These are the words of him who holds the seven stars in his right hand and walks among the seven golden lampstands' is a reminder that God is the Creator of the universe, who holds the nations in his hands and has ultimate authority over all things.

This was important for the Ephesian Christians who lived in a city that was renowned as a centre for the worship of Artemis, the fertility goddess whose image and influence were dominant in the culture of the whole region. This opening salutation was a reminder that there is a greater power than Artemis, greater than all the pagan deities, and that the One who was sending this message, was none other than the Almighty God known to Christians as the Father of our Lord Jesus Christ.

The seven stars are thought to be the messengers and the seven lampstands represent the churches who were to receive the message. The reference to the lampstands is an interesting reminder of the vision given to Zechariah in which he saw a solid gold lampstand with a bowl on top and seven lights on it. This led to the declaration, 'Not by might nor by power, but by my Spirit, says the Lord Almighty' (Zechariah 4:1-6). This was both a warning and a promise; a warning against relying upon human wisdom and human strength, and a promise of the power of the Holy Spirit available to believers.

The lamp was an important part of the household in every family and had been for hundreds of years. In Hebrew houses of the poor there would have been an alcove in the wall where the lamp stood, but in the houses of the rich the main room would have a stone lampstand about one metre high on which the lamp was placed that gave light to the whole house. It occupied an important central position and the lamp was kept continually burning. Its light signified the life of the family and the threat to remove the lampstand from the Church of Ephesus implied the snuffing out of the life of the fellowship. It was a strong warning that the whole Christian community in the city would be extinguished if the warnings were not heeded.

Words of encouragement

It would surely be perfectly logical that the Almighty God should know all that was happening in Ephesus, so it was no surprise that he would say, 'I know your deeds'. He knew all about them and the problems that they faced in a wicked city such as Ephesus. They had been working hard to share their faith with others, and they had persevered in the face of sustained opposition. Not only had they resisted wicked men among the pagans, but they had also had to deal with treachery in the Christian fellowship.

They had had itinerant preachers come to Ephesus, claiming to be apostles, men who had been making a living going from place to place sponging on believers and spreading false teaching. They had done well to test the doctrine and practice of these pseudo-apostles and to reject them.

They had also had to endure many hardships for the sake of maintaining their faith, even to the loss of employment and the refusal of pagans to trade with Christians. But they had persevered and not given up. They had shown great fortitude in resisting the pressures of neighbours, friends and even family.

Things not pleasing to God

The message would have been further heard by the Ephesians – that their courage and faithful witness had been at a price that they had not recognized. They had forsaken their first love! When they first came to faith they had embraced the gospel with such joy and life-changing abandonment. They couldn't keep quiet, they had to tell everyone the good news about Jesus. They had discovered the true God of the universe and they wanted everyone to know him and to share their faith. They overflowed with love for each other in the fellowship of believers. Their love was so great that they reached out to their pagan neighbours too.

They were challenged to think back to how they used to be and look at themselves now. They were morose and suspicious, holding firmly to their beliefs, but no longer with the joy they had at first. All that testing of false doctrine had been a strain on personal relationships and they had even been critical of each other in the fellowship, making false accusations.

However, the message told them that they were quite right to oppose the Nicolaitans whose practices were abhorrent to God and they were to be commended for this. They were quite right in perceiving the heresy in these false teachings and were right in expelling the teachers from the company of believers.

Timothy spent a considerable time in Ephesus. It is probable that his ministry came between those of Paul and John. Timothy had to face many problems in the fellowship due to the influence of the pagan world and

the impact of false teachers. Some of this was dealt with in Chapter Three, but for a full picture of the situation in Ephesus in the early apostolic period some forty years before John wrote from Patmos, the two letters of Paul to Timothy provide a great deal of information.

Message of warning

They needed, however, to recognize the hardening of their hearts that had resulted from all these bitter disputes and internal strife. They had ceased to love one another and they needed to heed this solemn warning 'Remember the height from which you have fallen! Repent and do the things you did at first. If you do not repent, I will come to you and remove your lampstand from its place.'

The emphasis was to be upon 'remember', 'repent' and 'return'. Just as God had removed his cover of protection from Israel when they turned away from him and he allowed his Covenant people to be overrun by their enemies, so God would remove his presence from the church at Ephesus and they would be powerless in the face of the hostile pagans surrounding them.

Promises for the overcomers

To those who responded to the warnings and heard what the Spirit was saying to the people of God there were wonderful blessings. Those who responded positively would find that the promise given to Zechariah would come true. The power of the Holy Spirit would enable them to stand firm in the face of all that an evil, aggressive, pagan society could do to them. They would be the 'overcomers' who would be given the right to 'eat from the tree of life'.

This was something denied to Adam and the whole sinful race of humanity. But the God of creation who held the power of life and death in his hands would ensure that his faithful ones, the overcomers, would be with him in Paradise, and would dwell with him, enjoying the fruit of eternal life.

Thus the promise of Jesus would be fulfilled that he would not leave his beloved ones as orphans, but would take them to be with him in the place he had prepared for them (John 14:18).

The ongoing relevance of the message for today

Christians at Ephesus were facing all the pressures and temptations of the pagan world where sexual excesses were legitimised and were even regarded as part of the religious practices of the local goddess. It was a highly materialistic society as well as one driven by superstition and fear of the occult.

In addition to all these external pressures, the Christians there had to face false prophets and heretical teachings brought to them by men who appeared to be authentic apostles. Many translations call them 'self-styled' apostles which emphasises the necessity for the early church, as today, to ensure the validity of its apostles and teachers. The Christians were always faced with the necessity to test all claims carefully and to weigh teachings by the plumbline of truth - the gospel brought to them by Paul and John.

The believers in Ephesus may well be described as 'vigilant but loveless'. They had lost their first love, the vitality and openness with which they had first embraced the gospel, the care and concern for one another that they had had in earlier days. This had gone in the battle to hold fast to the faith. Love had been sacrificed on the anvil of truth. That softness and tenderness that we associate with the presence of the Lord Jesus in the lives of his disciples had disappeared, leaving the hardness that could be described as 'righteousness without compassion'.

Christians today, throughout the Western world, are surrounded by similar pressures and temptations to those of first century Ephesus. Pornography and sexual perversions are everywhere in evidence, on television, video, film, and most insidiously, on the Internet. Superstition and the occult, including demonic practices, entice the unwary and lead many astray.

Within the churches in recent years there have been many false teachings and false prophecies that have disturbed the faith of many and brought division and conflict both within fellowships and between one church and another. The struggle to hold fast to the faith has been costly for many believers and has often resulted in the loss of personal relationships of love.

For many individual Christians and church fellowships the charge, 'you have lost your first love' is true. The call to repentance linked with the loving promises of great spiritual reward for those overcomers who resist the temptations of secular society and retain their faith and tender love has great relevance today.

> PERSEVERING BUT LOVELESS
> LOSS OF FIRST LOVE

Chapter 5

Message to the Church in Smyrna

What the Visitor Sees Today

Izmir, the modern Turkish name for Smyrna, is about fifty miles north of Ephesus lying at the sheltered head of a gulf extending some thirty miles inland. It has a natural seaport and an important harbour for exports as well as serving a fertile agricultural region of the country. It is not a city that offers anything attractive to tourists but its international airport makes it a popular transit city for holiday-makers heading for the beaches or tourists visiting archaeological sites. It is a huge highly industrialised sprawl centred around the Gulf of Izmir at the mouth of a river which in hot weather gives off unpleasant odours. Izmir is also a University town with a large number of students - hence although Izmir is the third largest city in Turkey its population is largely composed of poor workers and students. It is said to be the cheapest place to live in Turkey and attracts migrants from other parts of Turkey and wider afield. The city is expanding at a great rate to accommodate them as Turkey prepares to enter the European Union.

In contrast to the unattractive modern urban complex, Smyrna has a long and glorious history. The first known occupants were the Hittites who settled around 2,500 BC. The first wave of migration from Greece across the Aegean Sea to Smyrna was by the Aeolians, this was later followed by the Ionians. Homer was born here some time in the eighth century BC, while in 600 BC the Lydians conquered and destroyed the city and its fortifications. Theognis writing about 500 BC says that 'pride destroyed Smyrna'. It then remained as a group of small villages for the next 300 years until Alexander the Great defeated the Persians. He saw the potential of rebuilding Smyrna on the other side of the bay in the position it now occupies on the heights with their magnificent views across the bay. It prospered in this situation and has since then been an important centre of commerce.

Smyrna is by far the oldest city on the Aegean coast and is mentioned in the Iliad alongside Troy. It actually predates Troy, the remains of which have been discovered half way between Cannakale (on the Asian side of the Dardanelles) and the port of Alexandrian Troas where Paul received the vision of the Man of Macedonia calling him to take the gospel to mainland Europe.

Smyrna is renowned in literature for the beautiful architecture of this period that gave to the world the magnificent buildings, the ruins of which survived for many centuries. Smyrna became a strong ally of Rome and subsequently came under its control. Although it suffered in the AD 17 earthquake it was restored around AD 27 with magnificent large buildings earning it the title of First City of Asia.

The city acquired a highly cosmopolitan character with many rich temples to various gods and goddesses. In this polytheistic environment with the conflicting claims of different religions the gospel came as a breath of fresh air bringing with it an entirely new revelation with an authority lacking in other faiths that was demonstrated through signs and wonders. The Church in Smyrna was a product of this apostolic mission although in the eyes of the world the Christians remained poor, lacking the magnificent temples of the pagan religions. For the Christian visitor today Smyrna is attractive as one of the sites of the Seven Churches, but no one knows exactly where the Christians lived or worshipped.

Some eighty years after John sent the message to the Church in Smyrna the lower city was flattened in the earthquake of AD 178, which would no doubt have added to the suffering of the Christians in Smyrna. It is more than likely that the Christians were located in the lower city from which the great fortifications and magnificent buildings on the top of Mount Pagus with all its lights glowing in the night sky would have resembled a crown on the hilltop. When the Christians looked up to this as the violent persecution intensified around them they would have remembered the promise in the letter brought to them by John's messenger from Patmos that there was awaiting them a 'crown of life'.

In John's day the Acropolis (citadel) was located high up overlooking the bay on the flat topped Mount Pagus with its strong defence walls stretching down to the lower city by the harbour. There is some evidence of the agora (market place), that was the only part of the lower city known to have been rebuilt after the AD 178 earthquake, which is located half way down the hill to the port – but you need imagination even for this. It is difficult to find any significant correlated trace of the wealth and finery that made the city famous in past civilizations.

REMAINS OF KADIFEKALE OR VELVET CASTLE AT SMYRNA

Christian visitors usually ignore the lower city and head for the ruined fortress of Kadifekale or Velvet Castle which offers superb views of the whole modern city. Coaches toil up the hill through the narrow back streets of Izmir disgorging the tour parties by the ancient gates in the fortifications where a short climb up onto the walls offers splendid photo opportunities of the city below, the docks and the entire bay.

Christian groups often stand in the park among the ruined foundations just inside the ancient walls for a time of worship and for reading the letter to Smyrna. All western tourists are regarded by the locals as rich so they are quickly surrounded by local children offering a variety of goods for sale but Christians should beware of pickpockets. The local thieves particularly welcome charismatics who stand around with their eyes closed and their arms in the air presenting an inviting target! This is definitely a case of '**watch** and pray'!

First Century Smyrna

Although Smyrna was never a high status city like Pergamum or Ephesus, it was nevertheless important to the Romans and developed significantly in the first century. It had strategic importance as a port on the Aegean Sea and from there the Roman garrison could control the whole region of Asia Minor. Rome was traditionally tolerant of all religions, it was polytheistic in its policy throughout the Empire but there was an expectation that all its subjects would pay respect to the official religion of Rome that recognised the divine authority of the emperor. In Smyrna this was particularly important due to the presence of the Roman garrison in the city.

All citizens were expected, on a particular day each year, to visit the imperial shrine and acknowledge the divine supremacy of the emperor. The one exception to this rule was the Jews. They had been given exemption on the proviso that intercession for the emperor would be offered in the synagogues throughout the territories under the control of Rome.

The Christians were regarded as a sect of Judaism and as such initially enjoyed the protection of Rome. The account of Paul's missionary journeys in Acts shows a number of occasions when his Roman citizenship protected him. But as opposition intensified from orthodox Jews and the Judaizers who troubled the early Gentile converts, the apostolic mission to carry the gospel throughout the Roman Empire became increasingly difficult.

By the middle of the first century Paul was abandoning his practice of going to the synagogue first and was seeing his apostolic mission as being primarily to the Gentiles although he still believed in the principle, 'to the Jew first and then to the Gentile'. Paul's arrest in Jerusalem was in many ways a milestone in church history since it not only marked the conclusion of his own missionary journeys but he, as representative of the messianic faith, was officially denounced by the high priest and Sanhedrin.

Once the Christians were officially disowned by the Jews they had no protection. They had no national homeland and when the Jews denounced them and made specific allegations against them they were exposed to the full might of Rome. The sacrament of the Lord's Supper in which Jesus' words saying that the bread and wine were his body and blood were distorted by the enemies of the Gospel into accusations of cannibalism and child sacrifice in the Eucharist. From these accusations, rumours spread that the Christians were a secret society who were haters of mankind and as such were a threat to the Empire. It is easy to see how the Roman authorities came to regard the Christians as members of a subversive organisation that should be suppressed and why successive Roman Emperors carried out persecutions (see further details on persecution in Chapter Two and Appendix B for the list of ten particularly horrific periods).

The Orthodox Jews were enraged at the success of Christian evangelism and the large numbers of both Jews and Gentiles who were embracing the faith. They were outraged at the teaching of the apostles that this lowly rabbi from Galilee, who had been officially condemned by the religious leaders of Judaism and executed as a criminal, should now be proclaimed as the divinely sent Messiah and should actually be worshipped as Kinsman Redeemer, Lord and Saviour. Their jealousy at the amazing spread of the faith led them not only to infiltrate the congregations with informers, but also to make false accusations against the Christians and to betray them to the Roman authorities. They were, in John's words, a 'synagogue of Satan'. They were doing the devil's work for him and sending many innocent men, women and children to the unspeakable horrors of torture, public humiliation and death.

Not only were the Christians subject to false accusations being made against them by Jews, they also became the target of anyone who wished to bring trouble on them for personal reasons. The authorities often received anonymous allegations and to his credit the Emperor Trajan (AD 97–117) took steps to abolish these injustices. In a letter to Pliny dated AD 112, he said that anonymous documents should be ignored. His successor Hadrian (AD 117–137) in a letter to Minucius Fundanus, proconsul of Asia in AD 124, said that Christians should be protected from malicious accusers by having definite charges brought against them in court where they could be examined. 'If then anyone accuses them and proves that they are doing anything unlawful, you must impose penalties in accordance with the gravity of the crime; but if anyone brings such accusations simply by way of blackmail, you must sentence him to a more severe penalty in proportion to his wickedness' *(Bruce p 172)*.

John accurately foresaw the growing persecution that would take place in Smyrna; he saw this as representative of what was going to happen throughout the region and to the farthest borders of the Empire. He foresaw 'the hour of trial that is going to come upon the whole world' (Revelation 3:10).

One of the men who would have heard John's messenger reading from the scroll at Smyrna would have been Polycarp who may already have been a leader of a small church in the city. Early in AD 156 the aged Bishop who had sat at the feet of the Apostle John, the beloved disciple of Jesus, was arrested following an outcry of a riotous mob intent on anti-Christian activity. The senior Roman official who evidently wished to save the old man from the terrifying fate that awaited him said to him, 'Why, what harm is there in saying, "Caesar is Lord" and offering incense and saving yourself?' Polycarp refused to be persuaded but the proconsul tried again, 'Take the oath, and I will let you go; revile Christ.'

The old bishop then made his famous confession, 'Eighty-six years have I served him, and he has done me no wrong, how then can I now blaspheme my Saviour and King?' He was then paraded through the town and fastened to a stake and burnt. The accounts of this atrocity record that Jews from the local synagogue were amongst the most eager in throwing faggots onto the fire that consumed his body.

It seems strange that the Christians should have been so greatly hated when their whole ethos was not only to love the 'saints' but also to love everyone. A glimpse of what life was like in the Early Church comes from the Epistle to Diognetus early in the second century. It refers to Christians being indistinguishable from the rest of mankind in speech, clothes and customs except that they regarded themselves as having no permanent home on earth:

> Every foreign land is home to them, and every home is foreign …. Their existence is on earth, but their citizenship is in heaven … They love all, and are persecuted by all … As the soul has its abode in the body but is not of the body, so Christians have their abode in the world but are not of the world… The soul, immortal in itself, dwells in a mortal tabernacle; so Christians sojourn among corruptible things, while they look for the incorruptibility which is in heaven. The soul is improved when it is harshly treated in the matter of food and drink; so Christians, when persecuted, increase the more day by day. *(Bruce p.177)*

The Biblical Text (Revelation 2:8-11)

To the angel of the church in Smyrna write:

These are the words of him who is the First and the Last, who died and came to life again. I know your afflictions and your poverty - yet you are rich. I know the slander of those who say they are Jews and are not, but are a synagogue of Satan. Do not be afraid of what you are about to suffer. I tell you, the devil will put some of you in prison to test you, and you will suffer persecution for ten days. Be faithful, even to the point of death, and I will give you the crown of life.

He who has an ear, let him hear what the Spirit says to the churches. He who overcomes will not be hurt at all by the second death.

What the Smyrna Christians would have heard

Opening salutation

In the second of the seven letters, the message to the Church in Smyrna, the opening salutation, 'the words of him who is the First and the Last, who died and came to life again' came from the assurance given by Jesus to John when the Lord appeared to him on the island of Patmos. John was struck down with fear but Jesus said, 'Do not be afraid. I am the First and Last. I am the Living One: I was dead, and behold I am alive for ever and ever!' (Revelation 1:17-18).

Those who knew the history of Smyrna would have remembered that it had once been a major city that had died when occupied by the Lydians, but had then been resurrected to new life and status by Alexander the Great. They would also have known the emphasis placed upon resurrection by the goddess Cybele.

But this was also an important message for the Christians in Smyrna who were living in this sprawling cosmopolitan port city under the eye of the Roman garrison. Already they were under persecution and it looked set to intensify. The assurance that Jesus was the Lord of life, and that he had conquered death was just what they needed to hear. In fact, it would not be long in the future before their own beloved Bishop Polycarp would be paraded through the streets of Smyrna to be burnt alive as their most famous martyr.

The opening message was the reassurance that Jesus our Redeemer had already suffered the worst that evil men could inflict upon him. And God had not left him in the tomb, but had gloriously raised him from the dead, to be the first born in the kingdom of our God!

Words of encouragement

The opening greeting flowed naturally into the loving assurance, 'I know your afflictions and your poverty'. Nothing that might happen to you, or is happening to you, is hidden from your heavenly Father. He is watching over you constantly. The message from the Lord Jesus is, 'Yes, I know that you are poor in worldly goods and resources. But you are rich!' You can almost hear the believers in Smyrna protesting when they heard the messenger reading from the scroll, 'You must surely have got this wrong. We have no rich people here. We are the smallest fellowship of all the churches in the region and we have no wealthy or high status people in our membership!' Yes, but that is just what the Lord is saying to them.

In the world's eyes the Christians of Smyrna may be nobodies and they may feel that they have no-one to fight their battles for them. But God is with them and will carry them through. He knows that opposition has not only come from the pagan Gentiles but it has also come from aggressive Jews who hate to hear them declaring the Messiahship of Jesus. These men are a 'synagogue of Satan' being used by the devil to try to stop the spread of the Gospel. But in the face of all this opposition and affliction and although they feel themselves to be a despised little band of believers, they are standing firm. The weak are strong, the poor are rich, this is the power of the gospel that is turning the world upside down!

The Lord Jesus, the Alpha and the Omega, who knows the end from the beginning, knows what is soon to happen to his dear ones at Smyrna.

The persecution of Christians ordered by Domitian, Emperor of Rome, is about to break out with savage fury upon this little fellowship already known to the Roman garrison in the city. 'Do not be afraid of what you are about to suffer', is the exhortation from the Lord. 'I tell you, the devil will put some of you into prison to test you. And you will suffer persecution for ten days.' In fact, they were to suffer ten periods of persecution over the next 220 years, until the conversion of the Emperor Constantine in AD 316, but this message was probably simply an assurance that this present time of persecution would not last long. It did only last two years but was intense and cruel for that short period until Domitian was assassinated in AD 96.

Things not pleasing to God

It is interesting that this is one of only two of the Seven Churches not to have had any rebuke in its message. This may have been due to the intensity of the persecution they were suffering and their poverty, through which they had come to rely utterly upon the Lord. They had no other help, no other defender, and no other provider.

Message of warning

The only warning to these Christians already experiencing such pressure was that times would not get any easier but that God would be with them through the difficulties they were to face.

Promises for the overcomers

God's promise to them is exactly what they need at this time; 'be faithful, even to the point of death, and I will give you the crown of life'. The games promoted by the Roman garrison in Smyrna were popular with the crowd. The athletes who won the races were given a laurel crown, but those Christians who ran the race of faith would be given a more lasting crown that would be bestowed upon them by God and would keep them throughout eternity. Such a wonderful promise could not fail to encourage the believers. To know that a crown of life awaited them would enable them to keep their eyes upon Jesus even through the smoke and flames that would engulf them if they were called to martyrdom for the sake of their witness to their Lord.

The message that God was sending to Smyrna through the Spirit was one that needed to be heard in all the churches, 'He who overcomes will not be hurt by the second death'. The second death concerned the soul and the spirit, and it was the lake of burning sulphur referred to later in the Revelation (21:8) that was the destiny of the wicked. It held no fear for the believers in Jesus who were faithful witnesses for he would keep them until that day when he could present them pure and spotless to his Father.

The ongoing relevance of the message for today

The message to the Church in Smyrna warning them of persecution and martyrdom took on a frightening new relevance in modern history when in 1922 the Turkish army overcame the Greek army in Asia Minor. Smyrna at that time was a Christian city, as it had been for centuries under the Ottoman Empire, with a small Turkish quarter. The whole coastal region was largely Christian when, at dawn on 26 August 1922 the Turks launched their attack. After two days of fierce fighting the Greek army was in full flight and by early September Smyrna was surrounded.

On 7th September the Archbishop of Smyrna wrote an urgent appeal to the Greek Prime Minister saying that the entire community was 'descending now into a hell from which no power will be able to raise them up and save them...Out of the flames of catastrophe in which the Greek people of Asia Minor are suffering it is a real question whether when your Excellency reads this letter of mine we shall still be alive, destined as we are for sacrifice and martyrdom.' *(Smith M L, p.303).*

The Greek Government appealed to Britain, France and America for help but none was forthcoming. Two days after the Archbishop wrote his letter the Turkish Army broke through into the city, and the commander handed the Archbishop over to a 'mob of several hundred knife-wielding Muslims who took him to a barber's shop and mutilated him before killing him.' *(Fromkin D, p.545)*

Ten days of mob frenzy, of burning, looting and slaughter reduced the city to ashes. A correspondent of the *Chicago Daily News* wrote on Wednesday 13 September, 'Except for the squalid Turkish quarter, Smyrna has ceased to exist. The problem of the minorities is here solved for all time. No doubt remains as to the origin of the fire...the torch was applied by Turkish regular soldiers.' *(Housepian M, p.166)*

Did the message sent from Patmos in AD 95 foresee this further persecution of nearly 2000 years later? In fact, the events of 1922 were far more dreadful than any suffering inflicted upon the Christians in the early church by the Roman Empire. No doubt the promise, 'Be faithful, even to the point of death, and I will give you the crown of life' was just as relevant to the Christians in the modern era.

The gospel survived everything that the Romans could do to deter the Christians. The question remains as to whether today the gospel can penetrate the only Muslim country in Europe. It may be within God's purposes to bring Turkey into the European Union so that the Christian faith can once again be planted in that land and the blood of the martyrs can once again become the seed of the church to bring the message of salvation and hope to its people.

The message to Smyrna with its encouragement to the poor and the powerless will always be relevant both to individuals and to church fellowships in all parts of the world. As Jesus once said, 'The poor you will always have with you' (John 12:8) and there are many Christian churches in some of the poorest nations of the world that would readily identify with this message. The Christians in First Century Smyrna were 'poor but faithful'. They were surrounded by a hostile pagan population and many of their neighbours actively hated them without a cause.

This is true today in countries such as Indonesia, Pakistan, Nigeria and other communities where Christians live alongside members of other faiths who are strongly prejudiced against Christianity. This is also a growing phenomenon in western nations where hostility towards the gospel is evident in the secular institutions of government, education and other public sectors.

Increasingly Christians who hold fast to the injunctions of the New Testament are finding themselves at odds with the western world-view which is tolerant of all faiths but intolerant of any who claim particular access to spiritual truth. Any kind of spiritual exclusiveness or even objectivity is regarded as unacceptable in the increasingly secularised environment of modern western society. The stage is therefore set for the active persecution of committed Christians which makes the message to Smyrna highly relevant.

The message is not only valid for churches but is also a great encouragement for individual believers who are materially poor but spiritually rich. It is a great comfort to know that the Lord knows our afflictions and is fulfilling the promises he gave to the disciples that he would not leave them as orphans (John 14:18). The message of the gospel turns the values of the world upside down! The poor are rich, the weak are strong and those who have no status in the eyes of the world are great in the kingdom of God because they are sons of God (Galatians 4:6-7).

POOR BUT FAITHFUL
MATERIALLY POOR BUT SPIRITUALLY RICH
PAYING THE PRICE AND WINNING THE RACE
PERSECUTED BUT REWARDED

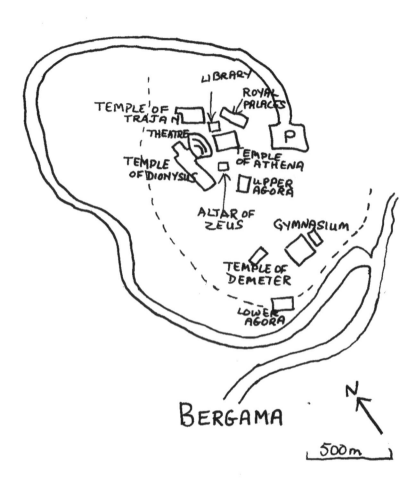

THE ACROPOLIS - THE UPPER SITE

Chapter 6

Message to the Church in Pergamum

What the Visitor Sees

Visitors to Pergamum, the modern Turkish town of Bergama, 65 miles north of Izmir or Smyrna, need to understand something of its history in order to appreciate the magnificent architectural ruins to be seen on the hilltop here with the modern city nestling in the valley below. Pergamum means 'castle' and this city was the ancient capital of Asia before Ephesus.

Mythology says that the founder was Pergamos the grandson of Achilles of Trojan war fame. The region was ruled by the Lydians, followed by the Persians who divided the area into the four satraps mentioned in Daniel, and came under Lysimachus. He realised its strategic location and turned it into a military base with somewhere to store his riches. The city grew to become one of the most beautiful cities in the east – with much art and literature.

The ruins are on two sites - the upper site or Acropolis being the Hellenistic city which predates the lower site founded in 248 BC on a fertile plain and built up by the Romans. It was important and strategic until the third century AD.

The Upper Site

There is evidence that the upper city was originally inhabited by the indigenous Anatolians some 800 years BC before the advent of Greek settlers but it was the Greeks who built the Acropolis during the period 281-133 BC. It was in this period, the Attalid era, that Pergamum became the most powerful city in the region and a renowned centre of Greek culture rivalling that of Alexandria and Athens.

The Acropolis with its magnificent ruins is a landmark which can be seen right across the valley. It contained the royal palaces, the arsenal and barracks, the theatre and many religious shrines. The impressive theatre seating 10,000 is built on the side of a very steep hill which has one of the most striking natural views in the world. This was very important to the Greeks so that the audience could have the full benefit of the magnificent vista. Even the stage for the orchestra was put up only for performances and removed immediately afterwards so that it did not obstruct the view of the countryside.

The Romans cared for none of these aesthetic things and built amphitheatres in the round for chariot races and gladiatorial events. Pliny describes two back-to-back semicircle theatres for performances which could be mechanically rotated to form an amphitheatre – this has aroused great scepticism. But it is true that the Romans often adapted the Greek design for more utilitarian purposes. The theatre at Pergamum shows good evidence of the adaptation of a Greek theatre to a Roman one.

The most important and oldest of the religious shrines in the Hellenistic period, whose ruins are directly above the theatre, was the Temple of Athena considered to be the chief goddess of the city.

TEMPLE TO TRAJAN AT PERGAMUM

Just below her shrine are the bare foundations of the great Altar of Zeus built during the reign of Eumenes II in memory of a victorious battle against the Galatians. This was the cause of much twentieth century controversy following its removal and reconstruction in Berlin in the late nineteenth century. For a number of years the Turkish authorities have been pressing for its return to Bergama.

The Romans built shrines to their deified emperors even higher up the hillside, the Temple to Trajan being the highest. This was begun during the reign of Trajan but completed by his successor Hadrian who also worshipped there.

Next to the Temple of Athena there are the remains of the famous Library which was said to house more than 200,000 scrolls. It was the most significant collection in the world apart from the Library in Alexandria. In 41 BC the Alexandrian Library was burnt down and Mark Anthony, wishing to ingratiate himself with Cleopatra, gave her most of the scrolls from Pergamum as a gift, virtually emptying the great Library at Pergamum of its most precious scrolls.

The Lower Site

Although the Romans moved their political centre of government to Ephesus, Pergamum remained of great importance within the region due to the significance of the lower site with its famous Aesclepium or healing centre. Visitors should note that the way to the car park at the lower site passes alongside a Turkish Army barracks with warnings not to take photographs.

Once inside the site the impressive colonnaded central approach road leads to the whole hospital complex founded in the fourth century BC although most of the remaining structures are of Roman origin. This was regarded as one of the most advanced medical training centres in the ancient world. The healing centre contained a theatre, a library, a temple as well as sacred springs with reputed healing powers. The whole complex provided a holistic approach to healing catering for mind, body and soul and included psychological medicine specialising in the interpretation of dreams. It is said that both Marcus Aurelius and Caracalla sought healing here.

There are various stories accounting for the origins of healing centres which were dedicated to the god of healing, Aesclepius, who claimed to have been healed by the venom of a snake. He then started to use snake venom as an antidote to certain kinds of terminal illness. The snake symbol

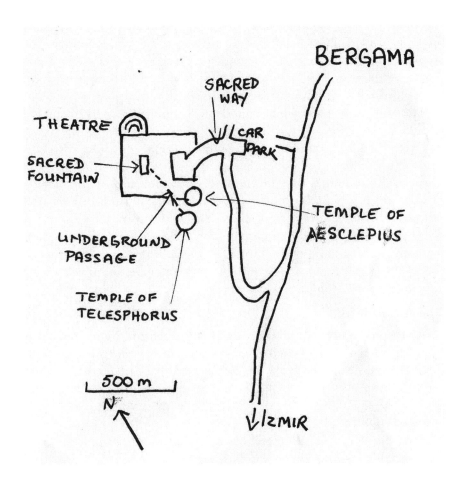

AESCLEPIUM - THE LOWER SITE

became associated with the cult which developed around Aesclepius and appears on the column at the entrance to the Aesclepium at Pergamum. The snake has become the international symbol for the medical profession. The reputation of Pergamum was enhanced by the waters of the sacred spring as well as by the various practices and healing methods.

On the main road between the upper and lower sites on the outskirts of modern Bergama there is an impressive red brick structure dating back to the Roman imperial era. It was originally built during the reign of Hadrian as a sanctuary for Egyptian gods which were popular in that period due to the presence of many Egyptian merchants. About eighty years after the conversion of Constantine the central hall became a church dedicated to St John. The church is said to have remained in use for Christian worship until about the thirteenth or fourteenth century when Islam dominated the area.

Today the striking red brick ruins of the church are surrounded by modern housing which also covers the courtyard, but the gigantic twin towers (one representing life and one representing death) appear well preserved. They can be seen by Christian visitors from the coaches as they drive from the Lower City to the Upper City to view the ruins of the temple complex on the hilltop.

First Century Pergamum

The first century Christians living in the great city of Pergamum would have lived in the Lower City where the great Healing Centre and medical complex was located. The skyline would have been dominated by the temple complex of the Upper City so that they were surrounded by the symbols of paganism that were formative in the whole culture of the region. In a central position on the Acropolis was the huge Altar of Zeus with its massive stone steps leading up to the elaborate altar with huge figures depicting the war of the gods with the giants - monsters with tails of serpents instead of legs. From the town below this would really have looked like the place where Satan sat enthroned – hence the opening salutation in the letter.

The Christian Fellowship in Pergamum must have felt constantly overlooked by this 'father' of the pagan gods. They would immediately have recognised the words in the letter. 'I know where you live – where Satan has his throne'. There was no escaping his presence in a central position on the mountainside, but also dominating the skyline at the top of the Acropolis was a temple to the official gods of Rome. This was the first such temple built in the Empire acknowledging the divinity of the Emperor. It was erected in AD 29 by Octavius when he became master of the Roman Empire and changed his name to Caesar Augustus, declaring his divinity. The temple was dedicated to Augustus and to Roma the goddess of Rome.

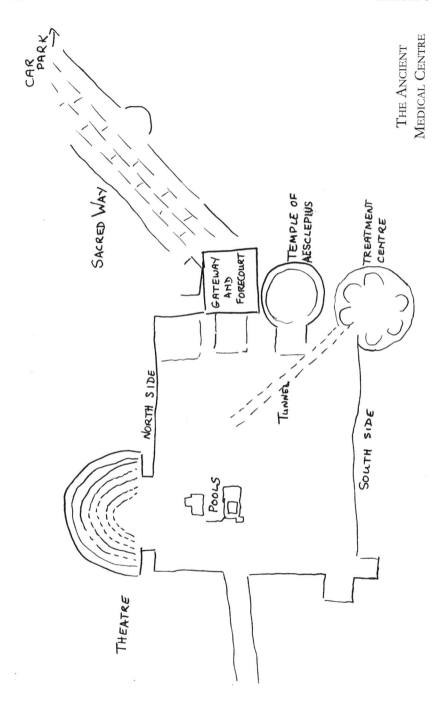

THE ANCIENT
MEDICAL CENTRE

Already, by the time John sent the messenger with the scroll to be read in the Seven Churches, Rome was being seen as the enemy of the gospel and persecutor of believers. Rome was doing the work of the devil in trying to destroy the church. So these huge edifices on the mountain overlooking the city where the believers lived in Pergamum must have seemed very threatening and oppressive.

One of their own number, Antipas, had already suffered at the hands of Rome in the persecution that had recently broken out in their city. He had refused to acknowledge the divinity of the Emperor and had suffered a terrible death that had left the whole Christian community shaken. As if that were not enough to cope with in terms of spiritual oppression, alongside them, in the Lower City, there was the famous medical centre to which people came from all around the world seeking cures for their ailments.

The effigy of a snake over the Pergamum medical centre would simply have been further evidence of demonic influence for the Christians and they would have associated this with the words in the letter 'where Satan lives'. They could not get away from him. He overlooked them from the mountain

CARVED SNAKES AT THE LOWER SITE

and he was alongside them in the city where they lived. They were surrounded by demonic powers and pagan practices that had an impact upon their daily lives.

In Pergamum, just as in Corinth, the Christians had to contend with the problems of food blessed by pagan priests. Paul's advice to the Corinthians was that although they knew that idols have no power over Christians and that there is only one God, it is sometimes not wise to eat food that has been offered to an idol or has come from the market where it has been blessed by pagan priests.

Paul says that although the food cannot hurt the Christian believer, care should be exercised not to allow their freedom to become a stumbling block to others (I Corinthians 8:9). He says 'Everything is permissible but not everything is beneficial. Eat anything sold in the meat market without raising questions of conscience, for, "the earth is the Lord's, and everything in it".' He nevertheless urges that if the Christian is in the presence of non-Christians who say that the meat is from a pagan sacrifice, then it should not be eaten in order to make a witness to the unbeliever.

It is more than probable that the Christians in Pergamum would have known his teaching because Paul would have given similar teaching in Ephesus. On leaving there for Macedonia on his third journey, if he went overland to Troas, as is usually assumed, Paul would have gone through both Smyrna and Pergamum on his way north. Unlike Ephesus where there was intolerance of the regulation, the problem in Pergamum was too much tolerance. They were prepared to turn a blind eye to anything, perhaps because none of them wanted to follow Antipas to the stake.

The fellowship must have been split between purists such as Antipas and liberals such as the Nicolaitans. It is, perhaps, somewhat unfair to blame Nicolas, one of the Seven of the Jerusalem Church, for the practices of his followers in Asia. It is believed that Nicolas had a lofty contempt for all things material. He was only interested in spiritual things, in feeding the soul. But this teaching could easily be interpreted as a separation between body and soul so that the material things or anything that happens to the body did not affect the soul. Human nature was weak and some of those who had been converted from pagan religions still visited the temples on special occasions or joined their friends and neighbours at special festivals where food was eaten that had religious significance which drew them back into the immoral sexual practices that went with them.

It could not have been easy to be a Christian in first century Pergamum with its centuries of pagan traditions enshrined in the magnificent buildings for which the city was rightly famous and with all the pressures to social conformity from family and friends in the community. This would have been especially difficult in times of special religious festivals when the whole city celebrated customs that had been observed for centuries.

The Biblical Text (Revelation 2:12-17)

To the angel of the church in Pergamum write:

These are the words of him who has the sharp, double-edged sword. I know where you live - where Satan has his throne. Yet you remain true to my name. You did not renounce your faith in me, even in the days of Antipas, my faithful witness, who was put to death in your city - where Satan lives.

Nevertheless, I have a few things against you. You have people there who hold to the teaching of Balaam, who taught Balak to entice the Israelites to sin by eating food sacrificed to idols and by committing sexual immorality. Likewise you also have those who hold to the teaching of the Nicolaitans. Repent, therefore! Otherwise I will soon come to you and will fight against them with the sword of my mouth.

He who has an ear, let him hear what the Spirit says to the churches. To him who overcomes, I will give some of the hidden manna. I will also give him a white stone with a new name written on it, known only to him who receives it.

What the Pergamum Christians would have heard

Opening Salutation

The opening salutation to the church at Pergamum significantly uses the phrase 'the words of him who has the sharp double-edged sword'. This image comes from the vision John saw (1:16) of Jesus with a sword in his mouth representing the word of God. The fact that it was the two-edged sword meant that the Lord not only had a cutting edge directed outwards but also directed back towards the people of God. Clearly there was something radically wrong with the teaching and practice of this fellowship that would be exposed in the message.

Words of encouragement

The message acknowledged that the fellowship of believers in Pergamum was right in a hotbed of satanic practices. '"You live where Satan has his throne'. That so-called place of health and healing with the symbol of the snake in the Lower City and the temples to the pagan gods in the Upper City surround you with satanic influences. But you have resisted the powers of evil and have held fast to my name. You even remained faithful through the fearful days of persecution that came upon you when my faithful servant Antipas was martyred and you were surrounded by violent mobs in the city streets. This was surely a demonstration of the spirit of wickedness behind the principality of Satan.

Things not pleasing to God

Nevertheless, there are some serious errors in your teaching that represent a real threat to the health and the future well-being of the fellowship. You allow people to remain in your fellowship who follow the same kind of practices as the prophet Balaam. He did not dare to curse God's people so he used others to fulfil his evil intentions. He encouraged the Moabite women to entice the Israelite men into sexual perversions and immorality. You too are succumbing to the same temptations in the same way by indulging in local pagan festivals and eating food that has been blessed by pagan priests.

Message of warning

You are allowing the spiritual life of the fellowship to be contaminated by these corrupt practices and you are endangering your eternal salvation by compromising with the powers of darkness in your city. Like the Ephesians you have the followers of Nicolas in your midst with their false philosophy of the separation of body and soul, but unlike them you are tolerating these Nicolatians. You think that it doesn't matter what you do with your bodies, that physical lusts will not affect your spiritual life. That is false teaching and unless there is repentance soon, very soon, you will feel the sharp two-edged sword brought against evildoers."

Promises for the overcomers

The final part of the message to Pergamum addressed to the one who has an ear to hear what the Spirit was saying was a beautiful promise for the overcomers. To those who had withstood all the pressures to idolatry and syncretism, the mixing of pagan practices with Christian beliefs, there would be a great reward. They would be given some of the hidden manna such as was put into the Ark of the Covenant during the time the Israelites spent in the wilderness when the Lord miraculously fed his people. In the Gospel John had referred to the manna eaten in the wilderness, which Jesus contrasted with the 'bread of life' that he would give to his faithful followers. The phrase also reflects the encouraging message in the letter Paul sent to Laodicea and Colossae. He said, 'My purpose is that they might be encouraged in love and united in heart, so that they may have the full riches of complete understanding, in order that they may know the mystery of God, namely, Christ, in whom are hidden all the treasures of wisdom and knowledge.' (Colossians 2:2-3)

The overcomers were also promised eternal life with Jesus. They would be given 'a white stone with a new message written on it' a name that would be so personal that it would only be recognized by the believer. The reference here is likely to be to the white stone which was regularly used to send an invitation to a special event such as a wedding and it would bear the name of the person invited. Here the promise was to the believers who would receive an invitation to the banquet of the Lamb and Jesus would use a pet name of endearment that the believer would readily recognize, but no one else would. It is interesting to note that parchment was invented and developed in Pergamum and would also have been white and books using this gradually replaced the scrolls. But the white stone would have lasted longer than scrolls or parchment!

The ongoing relevance of the message for today

The message to the Church in Pergamum is just as relevant today for Christian fellowships facing all the social pressures of conformity in a post-Christian society such as exists in many western nations today. Even things that were part of the accepted customs a generation ago can no longer be taken for granted. Social customs have undergone radical change in a single generation when couples who lived together unmarried were severely frowned upon. Today this is widely accepted and carries no social stigma, but the biblical injunction against immorality has not been repealed! Neither have biblical prohibitions upon homosexual practices been rescinded! But public opinion has changed in the face of relentless campaigning by pressure groups and society has become widely tolerant of both male and female same-sex unions!

There are numerous other social pressures put upon Christians to conform to the standards of a secular society that has no respect for Christian beliefs. The Name of Christ and God are regularly blasphemed in public on radio, television and film. Filthy language that would not have been tolerated in public places or in broadcasting a generation ago are today perfectly acceptable and Christians who protest are simply dismissed as being socially irrelevant.

The message to the Church in Pergamum was a strong warning that the word of God was unchanging and that he was watching how his people were behaving in a pagan society. This was both good news and bad news for the Christians. It was good news that God would bring judgment upon evil-doers, but it was also a warning to the believers who were not standing firm for their faith. Those who were prepared to compromise would discover that the sword of the Lord had two edges, one that faced out and the other that pointed back towards the believers.

How should Christians behave today in a post-Christian, pagan, secular environment that is hostile to the gospel? What are the limits of tolerance? How should the believer behave among family and friends who are unbelievers and who want us to join in revelries that compromise our faith? Can Christians maintain different standards of living from those currently acceptable in secular society? These are questions that face Christians on a daily basis in the post-modern western world.

If we are to take seriously the message of this letter, then we have to listen to what it says about the penalties of compromise, the warnings of judgment, as well as the encouraging promises. The promises are to those who overcome temptation and are prepared to face criticism and ostracism in family and community for the sake of the Lord Jesus.

PROLIFIC
POPPIES
AT
PERGAMUM

In order to enjoy the blessings and benefits of the Kingdom we have to be prepared to follow a lifestyle radically different from unbelievers. This means avoiding legalism but not compromising truth or condemning those who fall. This letter challenges the faith and practice of Christians today. Its warnings cannot lightly be dismissed for in so doing we endanger our salvation and the eternal life that is promised to those who are faithful to the end.

FAITHFUL BUT FLAWED
ZEAL WITHOUT KNOWLEDGE
DOWN BUT NOT OUT
FAITHFUL MARTYRDOM BUT UNCHRISTIAN TOLERANCE

Chapter 7

Message to the Church in Thyatira

What the Visitor Sees Today

Thyatira is not a tourist centre. It is a small modern inland Turkish town. It has had many names over the centuries but its current Turkish name is Akhisar. It stands on a crossroads at the intersection of two main roads running diagonally east-west and north-south, or more accurately, south-west to north-east and north-west to south-east. In modern Turkey it is on a main road between Izmir (Smyrna) and Bursa; and Bergama (Pergamum) and Denizli (Laodicea). Its geographical position leads to considerable traffic passing through daily.

The only tourists visiting Akhisar are Christians seeking to discover one of the sites of the Seven Churches. The church in John's day would, of course, have been meeting in private houses so it is not possible to locate the fellowship to which John addressed his letter. There has been no excavation of sites in this town to reveal the earliest of church buildings. There are, however, the ruins of a fourteenth century stone church building in the centre of the town and it is to these ruins that Christian tourists are attracted.

The ruins are located in a small square surrounded by houses and shops in the midst of the bustling little town. The square is fully accessible and open to the public. Coaches park in the square alongside the ruins and visitors used to be free to clamber over them and enter the nave of the church of which the main walls are still standing. The very fact that this site has not been built on in the town centre is a clear indication that it has, for centuries, been regarded as a holy site.

Early in the twenty-first century the Turkish authorities recognised the importance of this site for Christian tourists. They thereupon enclosed the square and provided a paved path from the coaches to an entrance. They have cleaned up the site and now charge an entrance fee. This does have the advantage of keeping the site free from local children whose curiosity used to draw them to infiltrate groups of Christians during times of worship in the ruins.

Little is known of the history of the church in Thyatira although clearly Christianity acquired considerable significance in the area for this large and impressive building to be constructed in the centre of the town over a thousand years later. The nave of the church that is built of stone is beautifully constructed and of considerable size. Christian visitors today are free to stand and pray in the roofless nave undisturbed. Increasing numbers of parties now come from western nations as well as from the Far East, notably Japan and South Korea. The Christians usually stand in the nave and read the message that John sent to the believers in Thyatira.

REMAINS AT THYATIRA

Surrounding the church nave are the remains of many stone columns and other artefacts including tombstones, indications that there was a burial ground here. It is these latter remains that have probably helped to keep the square as a holy site undisturbed by developers in the centre of town. The fact that there has been no excavation here makes it of considerable interest to Christian visitors who are free to use their imagination as to what was there in the past. Clearly the church was of considerable social standing for more than a thousand years after the writing of the letter addressed to Thyatira in Revelation 2:18–29.

First Century Thyatira

The importance of Thyatira in ancient times was that it lay on strategic trade routes and so it changed hands often in its history. Seleucis, one of Alexander's generals, when he conquered Thyatira in 301 BC, made it a western outpost of his growing empire. He then resettled many Macedonians into the city to expand it as a centre of trade and industry. Its connections with Macedonia continued for at least the next 300 years. This trade connection provided a link with Paul's ministry in Macedonia where he met a wealthy woman named Lydia in the city of Philippi according to Luke's record of Paul's missionary journeys. Lydia was said to be 'a dealer in purple cloth from the city of Thyatira, who was a worshipper of God' (Acts 16:14). Philippi was a Roman colony established by Augustus and Mark Antony for their legionaries after their victorious campaign against Brutus and Cassius who had assassinated Julius Caesar. As a Roman city it had no synagogue so on the Sabbath any Jews and God-fearers went outside the city to a place of prayer on the banks of the river nearby. It was there that Paul met them and agreed to go to stay in Lydia's home.

Thyatira's commercial activities included the dyeing of cloth. This accounts for Lydia's trade connections with her home city when Paul met her in Philippi, which Luke refers to as 'a leading Macedonian city'. The industries for which Thyatira was famous in Paul's day included clothing, wool, linen cloths, pottery, copper and brass.

In order to preserve standards many trade guilds were formed which functioned like modern trade unions insisting that workers in each industry belonged to the appropriate guild. In fact, there appear to have been more trade guilds in Thyatira than in any other Asian city. Inscriptions mention wool-workers, linen-workers, makers of outer garments, dyers, leather workers, tanners, potters, bakers, bronze-smiths and even slave dealers.

The trade guilds of Thyatira would each have held their own feasts and festivals that would have been linked to their own particular god. The entertainment at these festivals would often have been indecent, to put it mildly! The thing that made life even more difficult for the Christians was that each of these guilds was very patriotic and loyal to Rome. They demonstrated this by acknowledging the Emperor as "son of God" and incorporating the official emperor worship in their own religious ceremonies.

Before each meal at the guild festivals there would have been an acknowledgement of the divinity of the Emperor and any form of thanksgiving for the meal would have included an acknowledgement of him as their god. It was not possible for the Christians to engage in these ceremonies without compromising their faith in the Lordship of Jesus, but to refuse to participate in the guild festivals would have resulted in expulsion from the Guild which in turn would have made it impossible to follow their trade and would have led to unemployment.

None of the pagan temples of first century Thyatira have survived. So our knowledge of these practices has to come from writings of that period. There were plenty of Christians involved in the commercial life of the city and because it was a relatively small community, everyone would have known the other residents and there would have been a tight connection between members of each of the trade guilds. This would have made life extremely difficult for the Christians and it would not have been possible to seek anonymity or to opt out of the regular guild practices. At the time when John wrote the letter to Thyatira, persecution had not reached that city but his concern for the believers was that they were compromising their faith by their attitude of tolerance.

The Biblical Text (Revelation 2:18-29)

To the angel of the church in Thyatira write:

These are the words of the Son of God, whose eyes are like blazing fire and whose feet are like burnished bronze. I know your deeds, your love and faith, your service and perseverance, and that you are now doing more than you did at first.

Nevertheless, I have this against you: You tolerate that woman Jezebel, who calls herself a prophetess. By her teaching she misleads my servants into sexual immorality and the eating of food sacrificed to idols. I have given her time to repent of her immorality, but she is unwilling. So I will cast her on a bed of suffering, and I will make those who commit adultery with her suffer intensely, unless they repent of her ways. I will strike her children dead. Then all the churches will know that I am he who searches hearts and minds, and I will repay each of you according to your deeds. Now I say to the rest of you in Thyatira, to you who do not hold to her teaching and have not learned Satan's so-called dark secrets (I will not impose any other burden on you): Only hold onto what you have until I come.

To him who overcomes, and does my will to the end, I will give authority over the nations - 'He will rule them with an iron sceptre; he will dash them to pieces like pottery' - just as I have received authority from my Father. I will also give him the morning star. He who has an ear, let him hear what the Spirit says to the churches.

What the Thyatiran Christians would have heard

Opening Salutation

The opening salutation from the vision given to John on Patmos appears to be quite threatening in its imagery. 'Eyes like blazing fire, feet like burnished bronze,' does not promise a very soothing and comforting message. But John was aware that the Christians in Thyatira would have understood his reference to the prophet Daniel. He had probably often referred to this imagery when teaching in their fellowship.

The reference here is to the vision in Daniel 7:7-14, where the proud empires set up by men who boast of their achievements are eventually overthrown by the kingdom of God established by Messiah who is given authority over all earthly kingdoms. 'All peoples, nations and men of every language worshipped him. His dominion is an everlasting dominion that will not pass away, and his kingdom is one that will never be destroyed'. Far from being threatening, the salutation contains a wonderful promise that would be understood by the faithful. The message is made explicit in the promise at the end of the letter that the faithful would share in the authority given to Christ and his followers by God.

Words of encouragement

The message follows the same formula of beginning with words of commendation, 'I know your deeds, your love and faith, your service and perseverance'. There could hardly be higher praise for the fellowship. It may be that this commendation only applied to the faithful remnant at Thyatira, although it would also be a promise for those who repented of their wrongdoing. The message praised the fellowship for 'doing more than you did at first'. They appear to have been a very active company of disciples, eagerly engaged in good works, loving one another as the Lord commanded, showing great faith in the service of the gospel and even persevering in the face of many setbacks and disappointments.

Things not pleasing to God

Although everything appeared to be well on the surface there were some things that were being tolerated by the fellowship that were strongly displeasing to God. It doesn't look as though persecution had reached Thyatira, so there was a 'comfortableness' and complacency about their lives. They were busy in practical deeds but cared little for doctrine or going deeper in their understanding of the gospel.

The harshness in the warning brought by the messenger no doubt brought a rude awakening, 'I have this against you: you tolerate that woman Jezebel'. There was a false prophet among them who was not only giving false teaching but she was actually leading the faithful ones into sexual immorality and telling people that there was nothing wrong in going to pagan festivals. The message warned that if Christians ate food at these festivals they were already committing spiritual adultery and compromising their faith in the Lord Jesus. 'You cannot serve two masters'.

John may have visited Thyatira recently and spoken to the elders on this subject. Hence the strong message in the letter that this 'Jezebel' prophet had already been given warnings to repent that she had ignored. So her bed of sensual pleasure would become a bed of pain and suffering as judgment came upon her and all who indulged in her sins. The judgment that would fall upon her and her followers would be a warning sign to all the churches that nothing is hidden from the Lord. He is the one who searches hearts and minds and judges us according to our deeds.

Message of warning

The warning was to those who concurred, or simply went along with the false teaching of the 'prophetess' (or 'prophet' who may have been male or female, as the term 'Jezebel' could be applied to either gender) and who committed spiritual adultery with her by attending the guild festivals that adulated the local gods. They would suffer intensely unless they repented of her ways. Her 'children', or 'followers', would be struck dead. The warnings here may have been referring to sexually transmitted diseases resulting from excesses in the practices associated with these pagan guilds which would also have infected the children.

This underlined the need for all believers to recognise their responsibility for their own actions and the need to be able to discern truth for themselves.

Promises for the overcomers

Not all the Christians in Thyatira had succumbed to the enticing wiles of the false teacher. There was a faithful remnant who did not follow the prophetess and had not sought to learn 'Satan's so-called deep secrets'. Their reward would be that no further burden would be imposed upon them. They were not being held accountable for the sins of the rest of the Church in Thyatira. They had kept themselves clean and had exercised spiritual discernment. Nevertheless, they should continue to be on their guard and maintain their faith until the Lord's return.

This faithful remnant in the Church and those who repent in response to this message are the overcomers who hold onto the faith despite all opposition and trials and tribulations. Their reward will be that when the Kingdom is established they will be given authority among the nations sharing in the mission of the Messiah. In fact, their greatest reward will be their close association with the Lord Jesus. He who is the bright and morning Star will be their constant companion as well as their guide and protector. This is the message being conveyed to them by the Spirit of the Lord Jesus.

The ongoing relevance of the message for today

This message is particularly relevant to Christians in western nations where persecution is something that at present they only read about taking place in other parts of the world. Thyatira was a city enjoying great affluence where most of its citizens benefited from being part of a society that was at the hub of a variety of trades. There was full employment and most people enjoyed the material comforts that wealth could provide.

Nevertheless in order to enjoy the good life there had to be participation in the social activities that were part and parcel of the general life of the city. Many of the Christians saw nothing wrong in their participation in the activities of the trade guilds even though their festivities were idolatrous. They had learned the practice of tolerance in order to survive in a multicultural and polytheistic society, but in so doing they had compromised their faith. They were attempting to serve two masters and were thereby denying the Lordship of Jesus.

Many Christians in the western nations are facing similar situations that compromise their faith. We live in an age of tolerance where anyone claiming that any religion is superior to another is considered to be 'fundamentalist' - that is, subversive and possibly a threat to the security and peace of the state. There are many pressures upon Christians to conform to the culture and lifestyle that is acceptable to their friends and neighbours and those with whom they work. Christians often have to face difficult decisions in regard to the extent to which they conform in order to lower the social distance (or break down barriers to communication) between themselves and their neighbours.

It is never easy to decide how to be in a society but not of it, how to live and work within the community without sharing in its cultural values. These are very often decisions that individual Christians have to make for themselves in the context of their own circumstances. There are no easy guidelines but the message to the Christians in Thyatira is timely in its reminder of the dangers of compromise. Jesus himself warned that those who deny him will have no part in his Kingdom and will not be among those whom he would present to his Father.

FRUITFUL BUT COMPROMISED

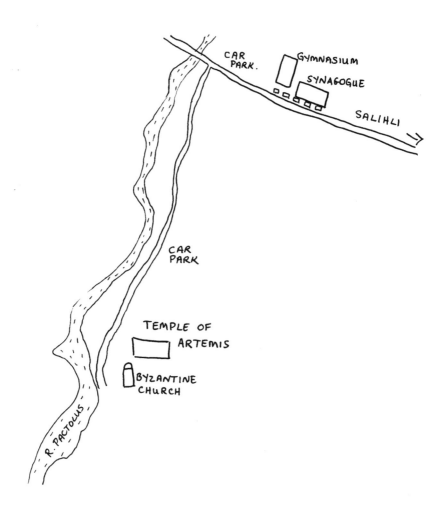

SARDIS SKETCH MAP

Chapter 8

Message to the Church in Sardis

What the Visitor Sees Today

The tiny village of Sart, near the modern city of Salihli, is the only sign of life on the site of the once great city of Sardis, capital of the Lydian empire which at one time ruled the whole Ionian peninsular including the great cities along the Aegean coast. Today, the ancient city is divided into two sites, North and South of the main highway.

The Southern Site

The coaches usually take visitors to the South site first of all where refreshments can be obtained. The two sites are surrounded by farms and the valley is famous for vineyards, olive groves and melon fields. The grapes are not for wine but for sultanas and at harvest time, in early August, children sell huge bunches of luscious sweet sultanas to visitors who patronise the wayside stalls.

The southern site is dominated by the ruined Acropolis which can be seen on the hilltop overlooking the Temple of Artemis. The ruins of this great temple have been partially excavated by an American team of archaeologists. It was refurbished by Alexander the Great and then by the Romans after the earthquake of AD 17. The remains of this once magnificent temple lie scattered around two towering columns with Ionic capitals. The temple of Artemis, like that in Ephesus, was built on a site originally dedicated to the Anatolian earth mother goddess Cybele whose worship was combined with that of the Greek fertility goddess.

In part of the ruins of the temple the remains of a church erected in the fourth century can be clearly seen. On the left hand side of the road leading from the temples on the northern side, there was another larger church from a similar period providing evidence of the presence of a Christian community worshipping here for many centuries after the days of Paul and John, but little is known of their history. There are, however, indications that the Christian community in Sardis was wealthy and influential. In 1984 the excavations revealed some ancient houses near to the ruins of the great temple complex. In these houses the archaeologists found many household items including what appeared to be children's toys. There were indications that these houses were the homes of Christians who occupied large houses with surrounding open courtyards and large water storage tanks. Clearly the Christians were part of a wealthy and influential community in the city.

The Northern Site

A more recent, and much more extensive, excavation has taken place on the northern side of the road to reveal an enormous Roman Civic Centre constructed after the great earthquake of AD 17 that devastated the city. This includes a magnificent gymnasium, baths, library, shops and an ancient synagogue. Josephus records that the Jews in Sardis had been guaranteed religious freedom from the fourth century BC and he mentions the foundation of a much older synagogue in the city.

MOSAIC TILE

The synagogue at Sardis is the largest known in the ancient world and, although it has no roof, sufficient remains to show its beautiful design and bear witness to its rich architecture. The floor still has elaborate marble mosaics which demonstrate the prosperity of the Jewish community in Sardis whose members held high status positions in the city government as well as in commerce.

The synagogue, which was located in the Roman Civic Centre, was built on the ruins of the old baths and gymnasium following the earthquake. It has an altar with the Lion of Judah and the Eagle of Rome at either end that can still be seen by the visitor. This was probably in recognition of the gratitude of the Jewish community to their Roman overlords. But it also indicates the social status of the Jewish community who were not only held in high regard in Sardis but were also fully integrated in society.

The synagogue is of particular interest to Christian visitors as it shows signs of Christian symbols (the *ichthus* sign) which may indicate the presence of Messianic Jews (believers in Jesus) as

LION AND EAGLE IN THE SYNAGOGUE AT SARDIS

far back as the second or third centuries AD. There are also clear indications that some of the shops belonged to both Jews and Christians.

REMAINS AT SARDIS

These shops are on the old main Roman highway and are located backing on to the southern wall of the synagogue. Visitors can see the excavated ruins of what was once a restaurant, Jacob's paint shop, an office, a hardware shop, and shops belonging to Sabbatios and Jacob who was an Elder in the synagogue. These are of great interest because some of them also have Christian symbols – displaying the cross.

From the entrance of the synagogue turn left and walk across a grassy area towards the imposing reconstructed courtyard of the magnificent gymnasium with its finely chiselled Greek inscriptions and serpentine fluting on the graceful columns. The gymnasium brought together the need for fitness in both mind and body. Behind this there is an ancient swimming pool and beyond that there are the ruins of a number of houses that have been excavated. These have been named the 'House of Bronzes' due to the many bronze utensils and other household items that were found. One of these houses has been restored by the archaeologists, replete with wall paintings depicting scenes of chariots and hunting birds.

First Century Sardis

Sardis was the capital city of the mighty Lydian kingdom founded in 1300 BC. The Lydian Empire reached the height of its power in the seventh century BC when gold was discovered in the hills above Sardis. This made Sardis the richest city in the world of that day. It was here that they developed the earliest known system of coinage.

In the sixth century, Croesus (BC 560–546), the Lydian king, who controlled the whole Empire from Sardis, lost the kingdom to the Persians in 546 BC after consulting several oracles including the famous oracle of Didyma seeking guidance as to whether or not he should go to war. He was told that there would be a famous victory and an empire would be destroyed. Assuming this to be good news indicating that his army would be victorious, he went into battle against Cyrus, who at that time was a little-known prince of a Persian sector of the Chaldean Empire.

But it was the Persian general who was victorious! In fact, this battle had a decisive effect upon world history and especially upon the history of Israel. Cyrus' defeat of the Lydian Empire enhanced his reputation and when he turned south towards Babylon the leaders surrendered to him before his army even reached the outskirts of that city. One of Cyrus' first actions was to release the Jews, who had been taken as slaves to Babylon by Nebuchadnezzar during the ministry of Jeremiah (BC 596 and 586), and allow them to go back to Jerusalem (BC 538) and to rebuild the city and its famous temple on its ruins (see Haggai 1:14).

The great Acropolis at Sardis had steep and almost perpendicular sides making it an almost impregnable fortress. Yet twice in its history its fortifications failed to defend the city against an attacking army. The first time the city fell was to Cyrus when a guard had carelessly left open a gate at the base of the mountain fortress that exposed a secret passage leading up into the city. This enabled an enterprising Median soldier to gain access to the fortress and open it to the invading army. The second time the city fell in a similar manner, this time to the Macedonians led by Alexander the Great who conquered Sardis in 334 BC, once again finding the guards asleep with the city gate unguarded and unbarred.

On each occasion when Sardis fell it was not due to the material weakness of its construction but to the human weakness of its defenders. Those who were entrusted with the responsibility of guarding the city by night were caught off guard allowing the enemy to gain access without any battle being fought – a point not lost in the message to Sardis!

Sardis was a great trading city on the main highway running east to west from Cappadocia to the Aegean coast. It was on the main road from Laodicea to Pergamum. In the first century AD Paul would have taken this road as he made his way westward towards Troas from which he sailed across to Macedonia. As Sardis had the most famous synagogue in that part of the world he is almost certain to have visited it. He would have noted its rich mosaic floor and beautiful decorative walls and ceilings. He could hardly have missed the Jewish-owned shops outside the synagogue and along the main road. Paul may have bought supplies there or even eaten a meal in the Jewish restaurant.

There is no record of Paul preaching in the synagogue but it is unlikely that he would have missed an opportunity to speak in such an influential place if given the opportunity. What is more than mere speculation is that either Paul or John may fairly be regarded as the founder of the Messianic community whom we know to have been resident in Sardis from the earliest days of the apostolic missionary era.

We cannot say for certain who first brought the gospel to Sardis but by the time John sent his messenger from Patmos towards the end of the century the gospel had also reached the Gentiles and there was evidently a flourishing Christian community in the city. When Paul went there about AD 45 the city would have been newly rebuilt after the devastating earthquake of AD 17. It received a generous grant from the Emperor Tiberius which enabled it to be developed as a thriving provincial Roman town. The large Jewish community in the city evidently shared the gratitude of the rest of the population and they showed that by incorporating the Roman Eagle on the bema (rostrum) of the synagogue.

The Biblical Text (Revelation 3:1-6)

To the angel of the church in Sardis write:

These are the words of him who holds the seven spirits of God and the seven stars. I know your deeds; you have a reputation of being alive, but you are dead. Wake up! Strengthen what remains and is about to die, for I have not found your deeds complete in the sight of my God. Remember therefore what you have seen and heard; obey it, and repent. But if you do not wake up, I will come like a thief, and you will not know at what time I will come to you.

Yet you have a few people in Sardis who have not soiled their clothes. They will walk with me, dressed in white, for they are worthy. He who overcomes will, like them, be dressed in white. I will never blot out his name from the book of life, but will acknowledge his name before my Father and his angels. He who has an ear, let him hear what the Spirit says to the churches.

What the Sardis Christians would have heard

Opening salutation

As with the other churches the opening salutation to Sardis is taken from the description of the revelation given to John (Revelation 1:4). The 'seven spirits' is a strange phrase that certainly should not be taken to imply a variety of spirits, or any division in the Holy Spirit. The simplest explanation is that through the omnipresence of the Spirit of God a personal message is being conveyed to the seven churches at one and the same time.

Words of encouragement

There are no general commendations in the message to Sardis, although at the end of the message there are some words of encouragement for the remnant who had not gone along with the rest. Not all in Sardis had gone chasing after worldly activities and soiled their clothes – and they are commended as being worthy. This faithful remnant whose clothes are clean will be invited to the heavenly feast. They are the ones whom the Lord will present to his Father in spotless white robes for they walked in his righteousness, not in a righteousness of their own that they think can be earned by much activity.

Things not pleasing to God

Instead of commendation the church as a whole is accused of having a great reputation for being a lively fellowship. It was bustling with activity but was spiritually dead. They are counselled to 'wake up!' immediately and fan into flames the dying embers of faith before the spiritual life of the church is extinguished completely.

The message to the church in Sardis in the letter read by the messenger must have come as a great shock to all its members and probably also to Christians in other cities where the Revelation scroll was read to hear that the church that everyone admired (including themselves!) as the liveliest in the region, was accused of being dead. 'Your deeds are not acceptable to God', they were told – they are incomplete and much is missing.

The church that everyone thought was the most alive in the area was said to be dead! By the standards of the world they were certainly alive, but in the eyes of the Lord their deeds had no lasting value. They could have been said to be 'worldly wise but heavenly foolish'. They were grossly lacking in spiritual discernment. They were warned to wake up and to open their eyes to see their true spiritual state before it was too late.

The message of warning

If you don't repent and wake up soon you as a church will have a similar experience to what happened to your city some time ago, when an enemy army attacked you, using a secret passage to breach the city fortifications. Despite the reputation of Sardis for having impregnable walls your defences were breached and the city was taken without a fight because the guard was asleep. This is what will happen to you Christians if you do not heed this warning and wake up to your true spiritual condition. You need to come back to the gospel that you first received and stop doing all those agreeable things that you enjoy doing but which are not advancing the Kingdom at all.

Promises for the overcomers

The names of the faithful remnant are already written in the book of life and will never be blotted out. In addition, the promise to the newcomers is that their names will be added to those already in the book. Each one will be acknowledged by the Father because they belong to the Son.

The ongoing relevance of the message for today

This message has special relevance for churches in the West, especially those in affluent areas. It is never easy to see ourselves as others see us and this is especially true in spiritual matters. It is not easy to see ourselves through God's eyes. We are all particularly vulnerable to spiritual blindness when we are living in comfortable surroundings and when the whole prevailing culture is highly materialistic. It is not easy to be in the world and yet not of the world. We readily become adjusted to the values of a secular society that exercise a subtle influence over us, and we conform to the lifestyle of our friends and neighbours, of those we work with, and whose good opinion we value.

This was what was no doubt happening in Sardis to the Christian community. It was an affluent city with a great reputation throughout the region. The Christians lived in large houses and were honoured members of society engaging in the world of commerce and taking their responsibilities as citizens of a great city with a famous heritage. The church was well esteemed by the whole city and had a great reputation for philanthropy and for lively social activity. Its members were no doubt proud of their position in society. There was certainly no threat of persecution because the Christians were seen as loyal citizens of the Empire who took a full share in all the secular activities in the area.

Churches in the affluent western nations whose members are living in an acquisitive culture need to hear this message. The values of the world are constantly transmitted into our thinking through advertising, through entertainment, through books, magazines, films, DVDs, videos and TV. It is very hard to separate ourselves from the prevailing culture in order to live our lives separated unto God. In biblical times the great men of God often sought solitude in the desert in order to be separated from the world so that they could communicate with God.

Moses was no stranger to the desert or the mountain top. Similarly the great prophets such as Jeremiah often left the city to be alone with the Lord. Elijah ran from the scene of conflict in Samaria and had his greatest encounter with the Lord in the solitude of a mountain cave. John the Baptist was more familiar with the desert than with the city streets of Jerusalem. Our Lord himself went into the desert to be alone with his Father at the beginning of his ministry. Paul also sought the solitude of the desert to think out the impact of his encounter with the Lord Jesus on the road to Damascus. For the great men of God in scripture the desert was not a place of separation from God, but of separation from the world in order to be near to God and to be aware of his presence undisturbed by worldly distractions.

The message to the Church in Sardis is highly relevant for us in the midst of the busyness of our lives. How often do we take time to be alone with God? For those who find it hard to hear what the Spirit is saying to the church today there is a simple question posed by this message to Sardis, 'What are you listening to? Is your whole life filled with the clamour of the world? What are the things you really value? Is it not time to take time out from the world and spend time before the Lord with an open Bible and an open ear?'

The answer to our need lies in the words of Psalm 46:10, 'Be still and know that I am God'. This is the word of the Lord. His solemn promise is that if we seek him with all our hearts we will certainly hear from him and he will guide and direct our steps. If we call to him he will certainly listen to us and he says, 'You will seek me and find me when you seek me with all your heart. I *will* be found by you, declares the Lord' (Jeremiah 29:13).

FIT BUT FOOLISH
MORE DEAD THAN ALIVE
DEAD AND DONE FOR
WORLDLY WISE – HEAVENLY FOOLISH
WHITED SEPULCHRES

REMAINS OF ONE OF THE PILLARS OF THE ROMAN CITY HALL
THAT BECAME THE PLACE OF WORSHIP AT PHILADELPHIA

Chapter 9

Message to the Church in Philadelphia

What the Visitor Sees Today

Philadelphia has always been a small undistinguished city. There was never a time in history when it had great shrines to rival those of Pergamum, Ephesus or Sardis. It was just a small border town with no great claim to fame, and that's how it is today. It was never a great trading centre, and it had no wealth or prestige to give it any significance in the region. This is very true of the modern city. In fact, it is just a small country town with no great archaeological heritage to attract visitors from afar.

Today Philadelphia is called Alasehir. It is just a small modern Turkish town whose only significance is for Christians because it is named in the Book of Revelation. Christian visitors heading for the ruins of an ancient church are probably the only tourists to visit the town. This building would have been there at the time when John sent a message to the Seven Churches although it would not have been used as a church at that time.

The remains of this building are located in a narrow side street that is difficult for large coaches to negotiate. The drivers used to reverse down the street from the town centre and stop outside the ruins of the Church. The Turkish authorities have recognised the value of the town as a tourist attraction for Christians. They have recently constructed a square with walkways from a coach park to the site of the ancient church.

Locally these ruins are regarded as a holy site and it is surrounded by a protective wire fence with locked gates. The keys to the gate are held by a local family who readily open it to visitors and treat them with great respect. The gatekeepers, although Muslims, have a limited supply of cards and Christian materials available in English which they gladly offer for sale. Visitors are left free to walk around the site and may take photographs. The remains of the church had not been excavated when writing this book and there is no doubt a wealth of artefacts beneath the grass-covered site.

The main interest in the visit to Philadelphia is to see the four massive pillars which are all that remain of the Church. These are literally huge and were strong enough to survive the numerous earthquakes that have afflicted this area. There is evidence of underground passages but these cannot be reached without extensive excavation work that has yet to be carried out. The building was originally of Roman construction and was built in the first century BC as the City Hall. As such it was probably the most distinguished building in the city. It was taken over by Christians in the fourth century AD and became a church which gives some indication of the status of the Christians in the area. For this imposing City Hall to become a place of Christian worship shows how the faithfulness of this little Christian community addressed in the letter from Patmos bore fruit that resulted in its growth in numbers and significance.

It is a humbling experience to stand between these great pillars and read the letter addressed to the church at Philadelphia. It is surely remarkable that these great pillars are the only things left of this great Roman building that was once the administrative centre of the city and the surrounding area. Then for centuries it became a Christian church. Is it just a coincidence that the promise to the overcomers in Philadelphia was that they would be pillars in the temple of God?

In the first century AD the Christian Church here was just a small and insignificant community when John wrote the message he received from the Lord. Yet the message was one of great encouragement that must have stirred the people to greater activity in sharing their faith with their non-Christian neighbours in a hostile pagan environment. The incredible success of their missionary activity is borne witness to by these massive pillars that were unshakable even by the devastating earthquakes that destroyed the rest of the city. This church could not be shaken because, like the little company of believers that also survived earthquake wind and storm, it was built on a sure foundation.

Visitors are warmly welcomed by crowds of local children, in our experience more than on any other site. The children watch for the coaches to arrive and excitedly gather to greet the foreign tourists. They love to have their photos taken with the newcomers and they take the opportunity of practising their English which they are learning at school. They often follow the visitors around the site listening to the message and offering their names and addresses for letters to be sent to them. There is an 'open door' at Philadelphia, the friendly city, even today!

First Century Philadelphia

The city of Philadelphia was founded by the Attalids about 140 BC. It was intended to give them a communication bridgehead into the central region of Asia Minor. It was located at the mouth of a long narrow pass on the main road from the coastal cities of the Aegean to the eastern provinces of Phrygia, Pisidia and Lycaonia. From its foundation in the second century BC its main objective had always been that of a 'missionary city'. Its purpose was to serve as a base for the Hellenisation of the regions beyond by spreading news and concepts from the great centres of learning and culture in the coastal region.

The city was at the extremity of Greek civilisation. It was sometimes known as Decapolis as it was one of a group of ten cities in the region. The name Philadelphia means 'brotherly love' and it was so named by Eumenes II in honour of his brother Attalus II and in recognition of the strong bond of brotherly love between them. Attalus II Philadelphus came from Pergamum, the city that was renowned throughout Asia for culture and learning, and he had a strong desire to bring Greek civilisation to the pagan masses as yet unreached in the rural communities.

The city was in a region often shaken by earthquakes - it was flattened by the great earthquake of AD 17, which also destroyed Sardis and Laodicea and most of the surrounding cities, and then again in AD 23. The city was rebuilt with the help of Rome through a generous grant from the Emperor Tiberius. It would have been newly rebuilt when Paul passed through this region and it may have been one of the cities on his itinerary although we have no direct word from Luke's account in Acts. We do know that Paul travelled extensively through the area of Galatia and Asia so it is quite likely that en route between Antioch and Troas he went through Philadelphia. Certainly we know that someone brought the gospel here in the apostolic age although it was evidently a small community of Christians to whom the letter in Revelation 3 was addressed.

In first century Philadelphia there were several temples reflecting the polytheism of its population. The largest temple, however, was for the worship of Dionysus who was regarded as the main god of the area. Greek mythology recalls that he was originally a demon who became elevated to the status of a god. No doubt the Christians of Philadelphia were well aware of this and they would have been able to discern his influence over their city and in the lives of their friends and neighbours. The letter addressed to them shows that they were a small group, but despite their weakness in numbers they nevertheless held firmly to the faith and did not deny the name of the Lord Jesus.

The Greeks regarded Philadelphia as a missionary outpost for taking their knowledge and culture to the heathen masses as yet unreached by the civilisation of which they were so proud. The Lord Jesus saw it as a 'missionary city' with a different mission – to carry the good news of God's love to the simple unreached village communities beyond the corrupting influence of Hellenistic culture!

The Biblical Text (Revelation 3:7-13)

To the angel of the church in Philadelphia write:

These are the words of him who is holy and true, who holds the key of David. What he opens no-one can shut, and what he shuts no-one can open. I know your deeds. See I have placed before you an open door that no-one can shut. I know that you have little strength, yet you have kept my word and have not denied my name. I will make those of you who are of the synagogue of Satan, who claim to be Jews although they are not, but are liars - I will make them come and fall down at your feet and acknowledge that I have loved you. Since you have kept my command to endure patiently, I will also keep you from the hour of trial that is going to come upon the whole world to test those who live on the earth.

I am coming soon. Hold on to what you have, so that no-one will take your crown. Him who overcomes, I will make a pillar in the temple of my God. Never again will he leave it. I will write on him the name of my God and the name of the city of my God, the new Jerusalem, which is coming out of heaven from my God; and I will also write on him my new name. He who has an ear to hear, let him hear what the Spirit says to the churches.

What the Philadelphian Christians would have heard

Opening Salutation

The opening salutation to the Church in Philadelphia is not taken from the description of God in the Revelation given to John, but comes in part from the first letter of John (I John 5:20), where Jesus is spoken of as the One who is true. The reference to the 'key of David' is to Jesus, whose genealogy was traced to Israel's archetypal king. The phrase 'what he opens no one can shut, what he shuts no one can open' comes from the promise given to Eliakim son of Hilkiah in a prophecy given to him by Isaiah when Jerusalem was under threat from the Syrians (Isaiah 22:22).

Words of encouragement

Unusually, the phrase 'I know your deeds' is not followed by a list of commendable factors and then things that are wrong in the church. The message to Philadelphia flows straight from the opening greeting into the promise, 'see, I have placed before you an open door that no one can shut'. The commendations are to be inferred from the statements that although this was a weak fellowship, probably small in numbers, yet the little band of believers had been faithful to the Lord and had not denied his name despite some fierce opposition from the local Judaisers who thought they were the only true believers!

As already noted Philadelphia was on the outskirts of the region. Roman influence did not extend far beyond Philadelphia in a north-easterly direction. The church was on the edge of uncharted territory and had been especially cultivated to extend Greek influence and culture in the region. Although there were as many as 500 Christian churches in the area that included the Seven Churches addressed in the messages in the Revelation, the gospel had not penetrated beyond Philadelphia. The message from the Lord Jesus was, 'I am setting before you an open door'. It was the door of opportunity for a missionary church to take the truth that they had faithfully defended into new regions.

The promise to the faithful ones at Philadelphia was that, as you reach out to others through the open door set before you, you will be so wonderfully blessed that the Jews who have opposed you will be amazed as they recognize the divine blessings you are enjoying. They will actually come and fall at your feet, acknowledging the love of the Lord Jesus for you.

Things not pleasing to God

Everything the church in Philadelphia was doing seemed to be pleasing to God. Philadelphia is unique among the Seven Churches in that nothing was found that was reprehensible or worthy of divine rebuke.

Message of warning

Philadelphia will not be immune from the time of persecution that is going to come over the whole Roman Empire, but the members of this little fellowship were not to be fearful as they would be kept through those days. Even though the Christians in Philadelphia were faithful believers this did not mean that they would be spared the times of suffering and persecution that were coming upon the whole company of believers in Jesus throughout the world. They were receiving advance warning of these times of trial so that they would be prepared to hold fast to the faith. Then no-one would be able to take from them the crown of life.

Promises for the overcomers

Messiah is coming soon and those who hold fast to the faith will not lose the crown of life awaiting them. The overcomers will be established so firmly that they will be like great pillars in the temple of God. In fact, they will be so closely bound to the Lord as part of the body of Christ that nothing will be able to separate them from the love of God that is in Christ Jesus our Lord.

It will be his name that they will bear, and as part of the new *spiritual* temple of God, the great company of the redeemed, they will be part of the new City of Jerusalem which God is creating that will come down out of heaven.

The ongoing relevance of the message for today

There are many churches today that see themselves as a small company of believers in the midst of overwhelming numbers of unbelievers. They see the whole culture of the secular environment as being hostile to the gospel. They feel powerless and insignificant in trying to fulfil their mission of bringing the word of God to those who are at best apathetic and at worst aggressive in their opposition. For those churches this is an essential and timeless message.

There are many individual Christians who feel isolated and unsupported. They have no church near them where they feel comfortable and they do not know any like-minded believers with whom they can have fellowship.

They long to have worship, prayer and Bible study with other Christians but they know of no-one in their locality. For these Christians the message to Philadelphia is essential and highly relevant.

The message is one of reassurance to the powerless and the lonely that they are neither of these things for the Lord is with them and he is all-powerful. This is a message of love and it is the assurance of the One who promised his own disciples that he would not leave them alone as orphans, but he would come to them and he would abide with them for ever.

Paul found that when he acknowledged his weakness he was not only strengthened but he could do all things through Christ. The Lord Jesus delights when his followers say how much they need him. He surrounds them with his loving protection and then empowers them as he did with the believers in Philadelphia. He set before them an open door. Even the most powerful opposition faded into insignificance as it did with the great city hall in Philadelphia with its massive pillars when it became a church. The tiny company of disciples discovered to their amazement that they had the power to turn the world upside down.

Philadelphia was established as a mission city to take the Greek culture out to the pagans in the regions beyond, but the Lord Jesus transformed the mission to that of taking the life-giving gospel to the world. As the Christians stepped through the open door, timidly but trustingly, they found the Lord going ahead of them, and, to their amazement, they saw the light of God's love radiate across the region.

The message is timeless. God has not changed. He is as powerful today as he was in the first century AD. The mission he gives his church is unchanged. It is still the Great Commission to take his Word to the world, to turn darkness into light, to release the captives, to set the prisoner free and to release his love into a war-torn world that believes that only the might of human arms can solve the problems of our humanity.

The message to Philadelphia needs to be heard by all Christians everywhere - that God empowers the weak: that he takes the things that are foolish in the eyes of the world and uses them to work out his purposes. He is setting an open door before his people today, before all those who will love and trust him.

> WEAK BUT FAITHFUL
> OPEN ALL HOURS
> WE NEVER CLOSED

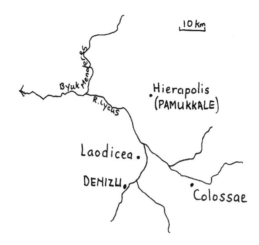

DOORWAY AT LAODICEA

Chapter 10

Message to the Church in Laodicea

What the Visitor Sees Today

Laodicea, the last of the Seven Churches addressed in the letters sent by John from Patmos, lies about 100 miles due east of Ephesus. It was one of a group of three cities to the east of Philadelphia and on the road to Antioch of Pisidia which was a major base of ministry in Paul's day. The three cities were Hierapolis, Laodicea and Colossae all situated in the valley of the River Lycus.

The three cities were closely linked geographically being within about ten miles of each other at the top, middle and foot of the same mountain and sharing the same water supply for most of their needs. Hierapolis at the top is some six miles from Laodicea and Colossae is a further three or four miles in the valley below.

Hierapolis

In Paul's day Hierapolis was known as a healing spa and it has a similar reputation today. The hot springs of Hierapolis still spill down the spectacular white calcium-coated cliff that can be seen from many miles away across the Lycus valley. It is one of the natural wonders of Turkey today and draws many thousands of visitors. Nestling down in the fertile valley below was the city of Colossae while midway between the two was Laodicea.

None of the three ancient cities exists today although there are extensive ruins at Hierapolis and Laodicea. There is a small working town, named by the Turks, Pamukkale, that is close to the ruins of Hierapolis. As a spa town it has many hotels catering for tourists and is the most convenient place to stay in the area since the hotels that were built in the 1970s and 80s at the top of the mountain have been demolished.

The tourist boom of the 1990s brought so many visitors to Hierapolis to bathe in the hot pools, or to clamber over the calcium cliffs that the whole area was threatened. In the interests of conservation the Government closed the cliffs to visitors for several years early in the twenty-first century. Only the Pamukkale Motel was allowed to remain open to the public with several hot spring pools within its enclosure. For a period during the alterations and restoration at Hierapolis, the hot spring calcium-laden waters that pour down the white surface of the hillside were diverted. It is this water, with its supposed healing properties, that has attracted visitors for hundreds of years. The constant flow of the warm water produces a cotton-like surface that glistens white in the sunshine and can be seen from miles away across the valley. But when the flow of water was stopped for a time the gleaming white surface turned to a dull brown.

Christians who noted this saw it as a parable. Without the constant flow of the Holy Spirit in the life of the believer, we soon become dull and lifeless, unable to reflect the light of Christ. Perhaps Paul had such a message in mind when he wrote to the three fellowships in Hierapolis, Laodicea and Colossae reminding them that in Christ they have been rescued from the dominion of darkness and brought into the Kingdom of light (Colossians 1:12-13).

Hierapolis has now become a national park and, although access to the pools is limited, visitors are free to explore the ruins of the city. Of particular interest is the spectacular Roman theatre that used to seat 12,000 spectators, built in two stages by the Emperors Hadrian and Septimius Severus. It was restored in the 1970s by Italian stonemasons.

Of great interest to Christian visitors in Hierapolis is the ancient Roman baths, an enormous construction that, soon after the conversion of the Emperor Constantine, became a Christian church. This shows something of the size and importance of the Christian community in Hierapolis more than two centuries after the letters to the Seven Churches. A considerable amount of the original building remains today and is well worth exploring.

Also of special significance for Christian visitors is the church closely associated with the Apostle Philip who is thought to have lived there with two of his three daughters. Papias, one of the fathers of the early church and a disciple of John was born here. He was the author of a lost work on 'The Sayings of Jesus'.

Hierapolis is the only one of the three ancient cities of biblical fame to have been extensively excavated. In addition to the impressive Roman baths and the well-preserved theatre the other major sites are the Temple of Apollo and an extensive necropolis which indicates the size of the population in its heyday. Many of these tombs have crosses in the stonework and reflect the Christian presence of later centuries.

Laodicea

By contrast to Hierapolis, Laodicea had, until recently, no work of excavation carried out. It has very little interest for tourists who crowd to the nearby hot springs of Hierapolis. In the 1990s increasing numbers of Christian groups began searching for Laodicea on pilgrimages around the sites of the Seven Churches. Turkish guides often did not know where the ruins of the ancient city were located as it was well off the beaten track. The best approach was through the little farming village of Korucuk, about two miles from which is a single track railway from which the city ruins can be seen, leaving visitors with a half mile walk to the site unless the coach driver could be persuaded to bump the coach over the tracks!

All that has now changed and the Turkish authorities have constructed a new road approaching the site from the opposite direction where some excavation has been carried out.

Laodicea was a very large city and its ruins are spread over a wide area. Parts of some of its impressive buildings remain standing although a number of the stones were used to create the railway! Only very limited restoration had been carried out by the time of writing this book and visitors are left free to wander around the streets and among the remains of the many impressive buildings.

Here you can examine the remains of the city gates and walls, parts of the spectacular aqueduct, the location of the great gymnasium and massive theatre as well as the agora and the acropolis. There are considerable quantities of pottery and other artefacts lying around on the ground but visitors should be warned against removing items from the site or buying coins from local men as this is an illegal trade under modern Turkish law.

Colossae

In even greater contrast to Laodicea, only the outline of the once great city of Colossae can be seen - and that only by those with some archaeological knowledge. The city stood on the north bank of the river Lycus, a tributary of the Maeander. It was a prosperous city on the great trade route from Sardis and was celebrated for its wool which was dyed purple and known as *colossinus*. It was the seat of one of the earliest churches in the region planted by a local man, Epaphras, who had been converted by Paul, and this was probably during his ministry in Ephesus.

Colossae was well known for a type of fanatical mysticism that centred around angel worship. Paul dealt with this in his letter to the church at Colossae when he emphasised the supremacy of Christ over angels and all spiritual powers, 'For by him all things were created, things in heaven and on earth, visible and invisible, whether thrones or powers or rulers or authorities; all things were created by him and for him' (Colossians 1:16).

Today, the whole area is under cultivation in the fertile Lycus valley but the raised area of the acropolis can be seen - so too can the general area where the remaining parts of the city were located. No excavation has been carried out here so the visitor can only see the outline of the area once covered by the city. Denizli is the modern Turkish town nearest to the three ancient cities and continues many of the industries for which Laodicea and Colossae were famous.

First Century Laodicea

The three cities of Hierapolis, Laodicea and Colossae date back to the Hellenistic period with Laodicea being the first to be built. It was founded by Antiochus II in honour of his wife Laodice whom he later divorced (253 BC). Laodice was a popular name for women in the Seleucid dynasty and there were a number of other cities similarly dedicated. The name means 'the people rule' - a concept popular in the democratic system of the Greek City States.

The founding of Hierapolis is usually credited to Eumenes II King of Pergamum in 190 BC in response to an oracle. The area was known to be a source of hot water – and poisonous gases. He is also reputed to have founded Colossae. Around 150 BC the cities of Hierapolis and Laodicea were linked with an amazing engineering feat by the construction of a unique aqueduct of large rectangular shaped stones with a hole bored through the centre, each of the stones cemented end to end. Some of these can still be seen in Laodicea. This pipe system carried the hot water from Hierapolis down the mountainside, so that the water was probably lukewarm by the time it reached Laodicea. This lukewarm water is no doubt referred to in the letter to Laodicea and is likened to their nominal faith in the Lord Jesus. Colossae also had its own supply of pure cold water which made the area very fertile.

Laodicea was a rich city with wealthy merchants engaged in the production of black wool material, and other cloth to make into garments. It also housed a famous medical school that was known to produce a special eye salve as well as specialised ear ointment. Again, there is reference to these in the letter to Laodicea. The city also had a considerable commercial reputation as a centre of banking and finance. The city fathers were clearly proud of their wealth and the strong spirit of independence that characterised the city. When many of its buildings were flattened by the earthquake of AD 17, Rome offered generous assistance with a major rebuilding programme. Laodicea, however, unlike Philadelphia and many other cities, refused this help saying that they had all they needed from their own resources - they proved their boast in spectacular fashion by completing the reconstruction programme in a remarkably short space of time.

In the apostolic age of the first century AD Laodicea would have been newly rebuilt and much admired by travellers as it was on the main road from east to west across Asia Minor. Paul travelled from Antioch to Ephesus and must have passed through this area although in his letter to the Colossians he writes: 'I want you to know how much I am struggling for you, and for those at Laodicea and for all who have not met me personally' (2:1). Of course, this may refer to those who had been converted since the Apostle's visit but it testifies to Paul's keen interest in the Christian congregations in this area. Paul says that it was Epaphras who had first taken the gospel to this area and it appears from Colossians 1:7 and 4:12 that Epaphras had planted all three churches in the area. In his closing greetings in Colossians 4:16, Paul refers to a letter that he had sent directly to Laodicea. He instructed 'After this letter has been read to you, see that it is also read in the church of the Laodiceans and that you in turn read the letter from Laodicea'. That letter has not survived.

By the time John sent the messages in the book of Revelation, Hierapolis was an important centre for the gospel and had its own Bishop, the most famous of whom is Papias, mentioned above, who also wrote about the origins of the Gospels. There are also historic references to Archippus, Bishop of Laodicea.

The Biblical Text (Revelation 3:14-22)

To the angel of the church in Laodicea write:

These are the words of the Amen, the faithful and true witness, the ruler of God's creation. I know your deeds, that you are neither hot nor cold. I wish that you were either one or the other! So, because you are lukewarm - neither hot nor cold - I am about to spit you out of my mouth. You say, 'I am rich; I have acquired wealth and do not need a thing.' But you do not realise that you are wretched, pitiful, poor, blind and naked. I counsel you to buy from me gold refined in the fire, so that you can become rich; and white clothes to wear, so that you can cover your shameful nakedness, and salve to put on your eyes so that you can see.

Those whom I love I rebuke and discipline. So be earnest and repent. Here I am! I stand at the door and knock. If anyone hears my voice and opens the door, I will come in and eat with him, and he with me.

To him who overcomes, I will give the right to sit with me on my throne just as I overcame and sat down with my Father on his throne. He who has an ear, let him hear what the Spirit says to the churches.

What the Laodicean Christians would have heard

Opening salutation

The opening salutation to the Laodiceans is drawn from the words they would recognize from the letter to the churches of that area written by Paul and sent first to Colossae, but also with specific instructions that it should be read in Laodicea. It was a reminder of the all-powerfulness of God who guaranteed truth, who was not only the Creator, but also the Ruler of the universe.

Things not pleasing to God

The message to Laodicea does not follow the pattern of the others; in fact, it is unique in plunging straight from the salutation to the accusation. The charge 'You are neither cold nor hot. I wish you were either one or the other! You are lukewarm' must have come as a great surprise to the comfortable complacent Christians of the great banking, financial and commercial centre of Laodicea. It was a city with a proud reputation throughout the region. To be a citizen of Laodicea was an accolade in itself.

When the messenger first read these words, 'you are neither hot nor cold', the Laodiceans may not have immediately associated it with their geographical position halfway down the mountain from the hot springs of Hierapolis. But the declaration, 'I am about to spit you out of my mouth' would have left them in no doubt. The lukewarm water was good for many things but not for drinking! It was a powerful metaphor illustrating their spiritual state in the eyes of God.

Message of Warning

The message that the Laodicean Christians would have heard was that they not only lived in an affluent city surrounded by material wealth but they themselves had imbibed the same spirit of materialism. 'You have not guarded the spiritual life of the fellowship' was the chief charge. They had become part of the culture of consumerism, driven by a spirit of acquisitiveness, 'the more you gain, the more you want'. They were just like their worldly neighbours and the people they worked with. They were just as house proud, enjoying their possessions, indulging in the same sensual pleasures as the pagan people around them.

The most worrying aspect of their spiritual condition was that they did not realize that they were 'wretched, pitiful, poor, blind and naked'. Pride and complacency had blinded them to the spiritual reality of their condition. What they really needed was not to increase the gold in their bank balance but to 'buy from me gold refined in the fire', true gold that would store up riches for them in heaven.

Moreover, they didn't need more beautiful clothes, the latest in fashion, designer models. They were proud of the soft glossy black wool that was farmed throughout the region and produced as fleecy cloth in their city. What they really needed was a simple pure white gown with which the Lord clothes his own precious children. They did not need the clever physicians of Laodicea or their potions such as the Phrygian powder famous as an eye wash. Their real need was to be washed in the blood of the Lamb and for the Lord to open their eyes as he opened the eyes of the blind during his earthly ministry. Then they would be able to discern clearly the pathway to destruction they were blindly following. Their faith would be tested in many ways.

Words of encouragement

Following words of displeasure, the message then proceeds to some of the loveliest promises in the New Testament. There is a brief bridge by way of explanation of the harshness of the charge against them, 'those whom I love I rebuke and discipline. So be earnest and repent!'

The reason for the heavy charge was that the Lord knew the potential of these dear ones. He knew their hearts and he was grieved that they had succumbed to the enticing riches of the world. They had been deceived by the spirit of Mammon that controlled their city. But if they recognized their condition and repented, allowing the Holy Spirit to fill them and empower them, they could be mighty disciples and great advocates for the Kingdom.

The believers in Laodicea had only to respond to the gracious and loving invitation, 'Here I am! I stand at the door and knock. If anyone hears my voice and opens the door, I will come in and eat with him and he with me.' The call was not just to the whole church congregation to repent, but for each individual to respond.

Promises for the overcomers

Those who did respond would be numbered among the overcomers. There is no hint of persecution here. Rome left the great banking and commercial city of Laodicea to order its own civic affairs, so the Christians had nothing to fear, except the spiritual corruption that was endemic to the whole materialistic culture around them. If they were able to overcome the temptations of affluence, they would be accorded the highest honour - that of actually having a place alongside the Lord himself; to be part of the great heavenly host of disciples who had fought a good fight and joined the company of the elect.

The overcomers would not only be the martyrs who had suffered death for the sake of their faith in the Lord Jesus, but those who had resisted the pressures of a pagan culture and whose lives had borne a good witness to the truth of the gospel. It is, however, arguable that John did not expect any of the true believers to escape the savage persecution of Rome. All who confessed the name of Jesus could expect eventually to suffer the same fate.

The message of blessing to the overcomers includes those who had fought a good fight against the heathen religions and their practices and those who faithfully resisted the pressures to conform to secular society and held fast to their faith. Those numbered in the great company of overcomers were one in Christ, having stood firm against the world and the devil, through the power of the Spirit of Jesus their Lord and Saviour.

The ongoing relevance of the message for today

The message to the Church in Laodicea is probably the most relevant of all the seven messages for the modern western situation. It depicts a congregation that is comfortable and complacent. They were well-fed and accepted the possession of wealth as the norm. The Christian community had accommodated their mission to the prevailing culture. They were not encountering any hostility because they were a challenge to no-one. The gospel they were proclaiming had no cutting-edge. The lifestyle of the Christian community was no different from that of their pagan neighbours. They were everyone's friend. They accepted and enjoyed an affluent lifestyle so they felt that they were able to do all things and they had need of nothing. They did not have to rely upon God for their daily bread, or for their protection, or for the means for carrying out the mission of the Church.

This is so similar to the churches in the modern world of the West where the nations have had the Bible for centuries and the majority of the population have grown up in a Judaeo/Christian culture where the laws and customs of the land have been largely determined from Scripture. The majority of the population in each of the western nations would say that they are Christians regardless of whether or not they are regular in church attendance or have any personal faith in God.

The church congregations themselves have largely lost their sense of mission, or regard 'mission' as something that happens overseas. 'Mission' becomes a matter of raising money to send others to carry the gospel to the heathen lands while the unbelievers in the great cities of the west, on the doorsteps of the churches, are largely unrecognised and unreached.

In one of the meditations we had on the site the leader drew attention to three modern songs of the late twentieth century which could so easily have been their motto - 'I'll do it my way!', 'Don't talk about love, show me', 'Keep on knocking but you can't come in'.

It would no doubt be a great shock to most practising Christians in the western nations to know how God sees them. If he sent a message today to the persecuted Christians in China or to Christians suffering martyrdom for their faith in the Sudan, Indonesia, Nigeria, or other parts of the world, God's message would be very different from the one he sends western congregations. The message to the poor and persecuted would be similar to that sent to Smyrna while the message to complacent comfortable Christians in the West would be more like the message to Laodicea.

Western Christians need to study this message carefully to allow the Holy Spirit to show us if we, like the Laodiceans, think of ourselves as rich and powerful with our wealth of material goods and our advanced technology that leaves little room for God. But the message, although designed to shatter the illusion of self-reliance and complacency, was not meant to crush the spirit of the Christians or to condemn them for having such resources available to them. Holman Hunt's well-known picture, 'I stand at the door and knock' (made famous by and linked to the wartime Christmas broadcast message given by King George VI 'I spoke to the man who stood at the gate of the year ....') is obviously based on this passage. The relevance is that there is no handle on the outside to open the door; the significance is that the response has to come from within - from us.

The charge that the Christians in Laodicea were lukewarm in their faith is also highly relevant for churches in affluent western societies. Any form of compromise with the world inevitably affects the quality of our faith and commitment to the gospel because it affects our personal relationship with the Lord Jesus. Jesus warned his disciples that we cannot serve two masters, compromise leads to corruption. The Apostle John had warned of this in his general letter to the churches, 'Do not love the world or anything in the world. If anyone loves the world the love of the Father is not in him' (1 John 2:15).

Peter strongly warns those who have accepted Jesus as their Lord and Saviour and who subsequently bow to the pressures of the world, thereby denying his Lordship in their lives. He says, 'If they have escaped the corruption of the world by knowing our Lord and Saviour Jesus Christ and are again entangled in it and are overcome, they are worse off at the end than they were at the beginning. It would have been better for them not to have known the way of righteousness, than to have known it and then to turn their backs on the sacred command that was passed on to them' (2 Peter 2:20-21).

Despite the strong warnings the Revelation message nevertheless gives assurance of the great love of the Lord for his people in Laodicea, 'Those whom I love I rebuke and discipline'. Unto whom much is given, of them much is expected! The promises to the overcomers in Laodicea are the most wonderful in all the seven letters. They are promised to sit with the Lord Jesus in his glory. This was something that Jesus even hesitated to promise to the Twelve! (Matthew 20:23)

The relevance of this message for today is that God wants his people to be different from the prevailing culture so that they can make a distinctive witness to the gospel. At the same time he wants those who are materially rich to use the resources they have been given for the advancement of the Kingdom. If we seek *first* the Kingdom of God and his righteousness we will have the right attitude towards material possessions and towards the right use of the spiritual gifts and natural talents we have been given. This will ensure that all are sanctified by the Lord and come under the direction of the Holy Spirit.

NEITHER HOT NOR COLD
I DID IT MY WAY

Part 3   What Can We Learn?

Chapter 11

Reviewing the Revelation

Overview

Enthusiastic students of the Bible sometimes overlook the fact that the Book of Revelation was written for the contemporary generation in the early church. Its message was conveyed in the context of an urgent topicality that was relevant to the situation at the close of the apostolic age. We do violence both to the text and to the message when we try to press it unnaturally into the context of later generations for which it was not originally intended.

The apocalyptic nature of the writing, particularly of the chapters following the messages to the Seven Churches, lends itself to prophetic interpretation that has a strong appeal to some Bible students who have a special interest in eschatology. Our concern in these studies has been particularly focused upon the messages to the churches, although we have noted that when John sent the messenger from Patmos the instruction was to read the whole scroll of Revelation to the fellowship in each of the seven locations.

When the whole message is examined in the context of prophecy it is seen to have both futuristic and contemporary elements, the combination of which gives it lasting value for generations far beyond the apostolic age. Prophecy can have more than one fulfilment and in the same way the declaration of the word of God into a contemporary situation will have lasting value for an understanding of what God is saying in later generations where similar situations exist. Herein lies the value of the messages to the Seven Churches with their warnings, exhortations and promises.

Some writers have likened the messages to the Seven Churches to seven distinct ages in the history of the church since the first century. These have been regarded by some biblical scholars as 'seven dispensations' with

Ephesus representing the persecuted church of the first three centuries and Laodicea representing the apostate church of the twentieth century and beyond. But this simplistic interpretation clearly represents the thinking of modern western minds and does not take account of the fact that the church in other regions is not in a similar situation. The church in China has been experiencing severe persecution since the Communist Revolution of 1948 and is by no means an apostate church. Neither is the church in Indonesia, Pakistan or Nigeria – all under persecution. Any attempt to make the message of Revelation fit into some modern dispensational theory certainly was not the original intention of the Revelation and we do violence to its message if we try to adapt it to our own pre-conceived theories.

Purpose

The Revelation given to John by Jesus was essentially pastoral in nature and was intended to have a practical application for the Christians at that time and to prepare them for what was coming in the near future. The message repeatedly refers to the expectation that the time was near when God would intervene in human affairs and although the days leading up to the great intervention would be times of severe testing, the believers should not be fainthearted because God would have the final victory.

The message was intended to embolden the timid, to strengthen the weak, to warn the complacent and to give reassurance to the faithful. John himself states the purpose as, 'The revelation of Jesus Christ, which God gave him to show his servants what must soon take place' (Revelation 1:1).

The intention was to explain the reasons why Christians were experiencing the horrors of violent persecution and murder. It was not intended to be obscure with a mystical message wrapped up in apocalyptic imagery, but to give understanding to ordinary believers in Jesus. Its use of visionary symbols, numerous references to the Hebrew Scriptures as well as New Testament themes makes it difficult for modern readers. But first century Christians would have had no such difficulty as they lived in a world of religious symbolism, pagan rites and festivities, Greek and Roman gods and religious myths as well as their own Scriptures.

Key to Understanding

For first century Christians the key to understanding the Revelation lay in the combination of pagan religious symbolism, an understanding and knowledge of the Hebrew Scriptures, plus an intimate knowledge of the growing body of Christian writings that were in circulation in the Early Church. By the end of the first century AD when the Revelation scroll dictated by John was taken from Patmos around the churches, the New Testament as we have it today did not exist, but it is very probable that all four Gospels were largely in their present form and were being widely copied and circulated from one Christian congregation to another. In the same way the letters of Paul, Peter and John were also greatly treasured and were widely circulated as itinerant Christian preachers and prophets travelled from one region to another, strengthening the brethren by bringing a word of encouragement from the Lord, as well as news of the progress of the gospel across Asia Minor and North Africa.

The Apostle John had had a long ministry in the region around Ephesus so he was well acquainted with the people and with their understanding of the gospel as well as with their language, culture and idioms. He himself must many times have used code language when referring to Rome and officials of the Empire. He would have had no difficulty in expressing the revelation given to him by the Lord Jesus in the kind of language and symbolism that he knew was familiar to the people.

This does inevitably present a difficulty for modern readers especially as *the Revelation was written in a way that would be intelligible to the elect but highly unintelligible to outsiders* so that if it fell into the hands of the authorities, the lives of believers would not be endangered.

The elect were in possession of the key to unlock the spiritual treasures contained in the Revelation. Over the centuries that key has been lost. Quite simply, we do not live in the world of Graeco / Roman pagan religious symbolism and it is not easy even for modern scholars to enter that mindset.

Relevance

Nevertheless, there is much that we can learn, especially from the messages to individual churches where we can see relevance to our own situation today. The warnings and exhortations as well as the promises have relevance in every generation, but it should not be supposed that the churches in John's day did not heed the messages.

Many people look at the current state of the Church in Asia Minor, modern Turkey, and conclude that the first century Christians did not heed the words of warning or they would still be there today. If that were true we would not have the gospel today as this overlooks the fact that the churches survived 200 years of severe persecution during which Christianity spread over the entire region bringing the gospel to thousands of communities.

The congregations were strongly evangelistic and missionary in character. They not only brought the gospel into the communal life of the towns, but they carried the good news out into the outlying villages and communities in the countryside.

There is plenty of evidence of the presence of strong Christian communities in the region for more than 1,000 years, right up to the invasion of Islam in the twelfth century. It would be right, therefore, to conclude that the Seven Churches not only heeded the rebukes, warnings and calls for repentance, but they stood firm in the face of wave after wave of savage persecution by Rome. Their faith was strong enough, not simply to survive as an underground community hidden from the authorities, but through their bold witness, courageous martyrdom and loving, generous lifestyles, they brought countless thousands to Jesus.

Their faithfulness enabled the gospel eventually to triumph over their persecutors and to bring the proudest heart in Rome, including the Emperor, to bow the knee to the Lordship of Jesus. It was the way in which they died as well as the way they lived that made such a life-changing impact upon people of all social ranks and eventually led to Christianity's triumph throughout the Roman Empire.

The messages need to be heeded afresh by each succeeding generation of believers in order for the church to survive - a living faith needs to be passed on. God has no grandchildren and believers everywhere need to take responsibility for passing on the message. Research shows that western churches are at their most productive and effective in the first twenty or thirty years of their life cycle (and many do not reach their hundredth birthday without being reborn or replanted) and many individual churches have come and gone. The western Protestant churches have not yet been tried over the same period of time as the church in Asia Minor – we need to heed the messages. There are many indicators that persecution in the increasingly hostile secular / humanist culture is only just over the horizon.

The messages place an emphasis upon the health of each church – not just on its numbers or its influence. Just as nothing can live in the Dead Sea because it only receives and does not give out, so our churches today can stagnate if there is no living water to pass on.

The regulations on entering Ephesus were likened to the different stages of entering the Kingdom from leaving the world behind, to cleansing by baptism, instruction and discipling so that we become good members of the eternal city and have a right relationship between believing and belonging.

Summary of the Messages to the Seven Churches

All the messages show that the Lord knows the deeds of his people. He recognises and approves the perseverance and faithfulness of those who hold fast to the teaching of Jesus and the Apostles. As a God of justice he rewards those who are obedient and faithful, especially under conditions of severe hardship, poverty or suffering. He also rebukes and disciplines those who are unfaithful and disobedient, whose lifestyle is inconsistent with their profession of faith, or who have lost their first love. He is particularly severe with those who are led astray by false teaching, and who get into adultery, idolatry and sexual immorality.

Repentance and Rebirth

There are particularly strong rebukes for false teachers and self-styled leaders who are not sent by God. They try to compromise with the world and deceive the faithful, leading them astray as did the Nicolaitans, the Balaams and the Jezebels. There are also strong words of warning for those who think they are righteous but are not living according to the Spirit of Jesus such as those who are intolerant of false teachers but whose spirit is hard, judgmental and loveless.

Additionally there are warnings about hypocrisy and self-deceit such as to those who have great reputations and are much honoured and admired by others but who are spiritually dead in the eyes of God, or to those who are rich in material wealth and social status but who are lukewarm in their faith. Urgent calls for repentance are particularly addressed to these Christians as well as to those who are unaware of their own spiritual poverty and are in particular danger because they do not realise that they do not have around them the whole armour of God and therefore they will not be able to stand when the storm clouds of hardship and persecution break with uncontrollable fury around them.

Strengthening

By contrast to the strong warnings and calls for repentance there are words of great tenderness for those who are weak through no fault of their own but who are struggling to maintain their witness under adverse circumstances, such as poverty, affliction or persecution. Others who are suffering through the actions of false brethren are given words to encourage and strengthen them. They are urged not to be afraid when persecution or hardships intensify, for the Lord will be with them to strengthen them and make them pillars that are immovable in the temple of God.

Praise

The greatest praise is reserved for those who remain faithful and continue to show love and increased spiritual maturity in times of trial. The Lord knows their deeds and he understands the difficulties and trials they are facing. He wants to assure them that they have not been left alone, that he will be with them and keep them in the hour of trial.

Although times of trial are going to increase in severity and will affect all believers, victory is assured for the faithful. They are the overcomers to whom wonderful promises are made and the love, the strength and the everlasting presence of the Lord is guaranteed. They are given the assurance that they will eat from the tree of life in the paradise of God. They will not be hurt by the second death and they will be given a new and everlasting name. Their names will be written in the book of life and the Lord Jesus will present them to his Father and give them the right to sit with him and to be with him for ever.

Bibliography

Early Church

Akurgal E, *Ancient Civilisations and Ruins of Turkey,* Haset Kitabevil, Istanbul 1983

Backhouse Edward & Taylor Charles, *Early Church History,* Headley Brothers 1906

Bell Mary I M, *A Short History of the Papacy,* Methuen & Co 1921

Benenot Hugh G, *Pagan and Christian Rule.* Longmans, Green & Co 1924

Bengel J A, *Gnomon of the New Testament Vol 5,* T & T Clark 1858

Bigg Charles, *The Church's Task Under the Roman Empire,* Clarendon 1905

Bishop Eric F F, *Apostles of Palestine,* Lutterworth 1958

Brown Raymond E, *The Churches the Apostles left Behind* , Paulist Press 1984

Bull Norman J, *The Rise of the Church*, Heinemann 1967

Bulloch J, *Pilate to Constantine,* St Andrew Press 1981

Cadoux, Cecil John, *The Early Church and the World,* T & T Clark 1955

Case Shirley Jackson, *The Social Triumph of the Ancient Church,* George Allen & Unwin 1934

Chadwick Henry, *The Early Church*, Penguin 1975

Clogg F Bertram, *The Christian Character in the Early Church.* Epworth Press 1944

Congor M J, *Divided Christendom.* Geoffrey Bles 1939

Cook J M, *The Persian Empire,* Dent 1983

Cushman Arthur, *In the Apostolic Age,* T & T Clark 1928

Dale R W, *The Jewish Temple and the Christian Church*, Hodder & Stoughton 1870

Danielou J & Marrou H, *The Christian Centuries Vol 1*, DLT 1983

Davies J G, *The Making of the Church,* Mowbray 1983

De Pressense E, *The Early Years of Christianity Vol 4*, H & S 1892

Dollinger John J I, *The First Age of Christianity and the Church*, Gibbings and Co 1906

Edmundsen George, *The Church in Rome in the First Century*, Longmans, Green & Co 1913

Every George, *Understanding Eastern Christianity*, SCM Press 1980

Ferguson John, *The Religions of the Roman Empire,* Thames & Hudson 1982

Foakes, J F J, *The History of the Christian Church to AD 461*, George Allen & Unwin 1942

Fox Robin Lane, *Pagans & Christians,* Penguin 1986

Frend W H C, *The Rise of Christianity,* Darton, Longman & Todd 1984

Frend W H C, *The Early Church from the beginning to 461,* SCM Press 1982

Glover T R, *The Conflict of Religions in the Early Roman Empire*, Methuen & Co 1923

Goppelt Leonhard, *Apostolic and Post-Apostolic Times*, Adam & Charles Black 1970

Gough Michael, *The Early Christians*, Thames & Hudson 1961

Gwatkin H M, *Early Church History to AD 313 Vol 1*, Macmillan & Co 1909

Gwatkin H M, *Selections from Early Christian Writers*, Macmillan 1920

Hemer Colin J, *The Letters to the Seven Churches of Asia*, Eerdmans 1989

Henshaw T, *The Foundation of the Christian Church*, George Gill & Sons

Heron James, *The Evolution of Latin Christianity*, James Clarke & Co, 1919

Hoehner Harold W, *Herod Antipas*, Zondervan 1980

John of Bristol, *Ecclesiastical History of the Second and Third Century*, Griffith Farran & Co

Jones A H M, *Constantine & The Conversion of Rome*, Pelican 1972

Kee Howard Clark, *The Origins of Christianity*, SPCK 1973

Keith Khodadad E, *The Social Life of a Jew in the Time of Christ*, CMJ 1959

Kenyon Kathleen M, *The Bible & Recent Archaeology*, Colonnade 1978

Kidd BJ, *A History of the Church to AD461*, Oxford 1922

Kidd BJ, *The Roman Primacy to AD 461*, SPCK 1936

Latourette K S, *A History of Christianity Vol 1*, Harper & Row 1975

Latourette K S, *A History of the Expansion of Christianity Vol 1*, Eyre & Spottiswoode 1938

Levison N, *The Jewish Background of Christianity*, T & T Clark 1932

Lietzmann Hans, *The Era of the Church Fathers*, Lutterworth, 1951

Lietzmann Hans, *The Founding of the Church Universal*, Nicholson & Watson 1938

MacGregor G H C & Purdy A C, *Jew & Greek Tutors unto Christ*, Nicholson & Watson 1936

Magnus Laurie, *The Jews in the Christian Era*, Ernest Benn Ltd 1929

Martin Malachi, *The Decline and Fall of the Roman Church*, Secher & Warburg 1981

McGiffert, *History of Christianity*

Meeks Wayne A, *The First Urban Christians*, Yale University Press 1983

Morris Leon, *Revelation*, IVP 1976

Puller F W, *The Primitive Saints and the See of Rome*, Longmans, Green & Co 1914

Rainey Robert, *The Ancient Catholic Church*, T & T Clark 1913

Robertson J M, *A Short History of Christianity*, Watts & Co 1937

Ropes James Hardy *The Apostolic Age*, Charles Scribner's Sons 1906

Rousselot Pierre, *The Life of the Church*, Sheed & Ward 1934

Russell D S, *From Early Judaism to Early Church*, SCM Press 1986

Sawyer John F A, *From Moses to Patmos,* SPCK 1977

Schofield J N, *The Historical Background to the Bible,* Thomas Nelson and Sons 1948

Schofield J N, *The Religious Background of the Bible,* Thomas Nelson and Sons 1944

Shaw Desmond, *Jesus or Paul?,* Skeffington & Son

Stanley A P, *The Jewish Church Vol 3,* John Murray 1876

Stevenson J (ed), *A New Eusebius,* SPCK 1977

Stone Darwell, *The Christian Church,* Rivingtons 1905

Wand J W C, *A History of the Early Church to AD 500,* Methuen & Co 1977

Watkins H M G (ed), *The Church Past & Present,* James Nisbet & Co 1900

Welsford A E, *Life in the Early Church,* SPCK 1951

Whitham A R, *History of the Christian Church,* Rivingtons 1936

Workman H B, *Persecution in the Early Church,* Charles H Kelly 1906

Modern Period

Fromkin David, *A Peace To End All Peace: The Fall of the Ottoman Empire and the Creation of the Modern Middle East,* Phoenix Press, London 2003

Housepian Marjorie, *Smyrna 1922: The Destruction of a City,* Faber, London 1972

Llewellyn, *Greece in Asia Minor, 1919 – 1922,* New York 1973

Smith Michael, *Ionian Vision,* St Martin's Press

Appendix A

Time Lines and Civilisations

BC 7500   Earliest known inhabitants; earliest human community at
                 Catal Hoyik Hattis

Stone and Copper Age (c 5,000 – 3,000 BC)

BC 5000   Settlement at Hacilar

Bronze Age (c 3,000 – 1,200 BC)

BC 2600-1900   Proto-Hittite Empire in central and south-eastern Anatolia
BC 1900-1300   Hittite Empire, wars with Egypt; the Patriarch Abraham
                 departs from Haran, near Sanifurfa, for Canaan
BC 1250   Trojan War

Anatolian Dark Ages (c 1,200 – c 750 BC)

BC 1200-600   Phrygian and Mycean invasions, followed by the great
                 period of Hellenic civilisation; Yassi Hoyuk settlement
                 flourishes; King Midas and King Croesus reign; coinage
                 is invented; kingdoms of Ionia, Lycia, Lydia, Caria,
                 Pamphylia; Empire of Urartu

Archaic Period (c750 – 479 BC)

BC c750 – 700   Greek Literature including Homer

Classical Period (479 - 323 BC)

BC 550   Cyrus of Persia invades Anatolia
BC 334   Conquest of simply everything and everybody by
                 Alexander the Great from Macedonia

Hellenistic Period (323 – 130 BC)

BC 279   Celts (or Gauls) invade and set up Galatia near Ankara
BC 250   Rise of the Kingdom of Pergamum (Bergama)

Roman Period (129 BC – AD 330)

BC 129   Rome establishes the Province of Asia ('Asia Minor'), with its capital at Ephesus (near Izmir)

AD 47-57   St Paul's travels in Anatolia

Byzantine Period (330 – 1453)

AD 330   Constantine dedicates the 'New Rome' of Constantinople, and the centre of the Empire moves from Rome to the Bosphorus

AD 527-65   Reign of Justinian, greatest Byzantine emperor; construction of Sancta Sophia, greatest church in the world

AD 570-622   Muhammed's birth; revelation of the Koran; flight (hyra) to Medina

AD 1037-1109   Empire of the Great Seljuk Turks, based in Iran

Seljuk Period

AD 1071-1243   Seljuk Sultanate of Rum, based in Konya; life and work of Ceialeddin Rumi (Weviana l, founder of the Whirling Dervishes).

AD 1000s-1200s Age of the Crusades

Ottoman Period

AD 1288   Birth of the Ottoman Empire, near Bursa

AD 1453   Conquest of Constantinople by Mehmet II

AD 1520-66   Reign of Sultan Suleyman the Magnificent, the great age of the Ottoman Empire; most of North Africa, most of Eastern Europe and all of the Middle East controlled from Istanbul; Ottoman navies patrol the Mediterranean and Red Seas and the Indian Ocean

AD 1876-1909   Reign of Sultan Abdul Hamit, last of the powerful sultans; the 'Eastern Question' arises: which European nations will be able to grab Ottoman territory when the Empire topples?

Republic of Turkey (1923 – on-going)

AD 1923   Proclamation of the Turkish Republic

AD 1938   Death of Ataturk

Appendix B

10 Major Periods of Persecution
linked with 10 Roman Emperors

AD 64 - 68   NERO (lived 37–68; Emperor 54–68)
The first Emperor to persecute Christians

AD 94 - 96   DOMITIAN (lived 52–96; Emperor 81–96)
John Exiled to Patmos, Christians in Ephesus persecuted

AD 104 - 117   TRAJAN (lived 53–117; Emperor 97–117)
Ignatius burned at the stake

AD 117 - 137   HADRIAN (lived 76–138; Emperor 117–137)
Apostolic Fathers persecuted, Clement, Bishop of Rome,
executed

AD 161 - 180   MARCUS AURELIUS (lived 121–180; Emperor 161-80)
Polycarp, Bishop of Smyrna martyred

AD 200 - 211   SEVERUS (lived 146–211; Emperor 183–211)
Christians throughout the Roman Empire persecuted

AD 235 - 238   MAXIMINUS (lived 200–238; Emperor 235–238)

AD 250 - 253   DECIUS (lived 201–251; Emperor 249–251)
Severe persecution

AD 257 - 269   VALERIANUS (lived 193–260; Emperor 253–260)
Bishop Pion burned at the stake and Camprian slain

AD 303 - 313   DIOCLETIAN (lived 245–313; Emperor 284–305,
abdicated); the worst Emperor, who attempted to
exterminate the Christian faith

The Moggerhanger Experience

Moggerhanger Park is home to a community of Christian ministries who are in a covenant relationship with each other, sharing resources, supporting each other and upholding each other in prayer. Together these ministries continue to serve the nation in the kind of ethos of those who were connected with the house 200 years ago.

From the middle of the 18th century Moggerhanger Park was owned by the Thornton family - related to the Wilberforce family. The house was owned by Godfrey Thornton who was a director of the Bank of England and became governor in 1793. His cousin, Henry Thornton was MP for Southwark and one of the leaders of the so-called Clapham Sect, the group of evangelical Christians who were foremost in the campaign for the abolition of slavery and whose tireless work paved the way for a variety of social, economic and moral reforms in the pre-Victorian period.

In 1790 Godfrey Thornton engaged Sir John Soane who had built the first Bank of England to enlarge and improve his house at Moggerhanger. Soane knocked down most of the old Tudor house and completely redesigned it. Thornton also engaged Humphry Repton, the foremost landscape gardener of his day, to design and layout the estate including the parkland, pleasure garden, orchard, walled gardens and woods.

The ministries at Moggerhanger who acquired the house in 1994 set up a preservation trust when the house was upgraded to Grade One in 1997 to carry out a full restoration programme using Soane's original plans now stored in the Soane Museum in Lincoln's Inn Field, London.

The Centre for Contemporary Ministry (CCM) is the ministry that coordinates the joint work of the other ministries and oversees the links with Moggerhanger House Preservation Trust and Moggerhanger Park Ltd, the team responsible for the running and operation of the house. CCM was responsible for the founding of Clapham Connections, the Thornton Institute for Business Ethics, the Christian Workplace Forum and *transform-uk* and of The Family Matters Institute which is now an independent charity;.

Each of these ministries follows a similar strategy of Christian mission to that established by Wilberforce and Thornton and members of the Clapham group that included pioneers such as Henry Venn, the vicar of Clapham Parish Church who led the way in social welfare and Hannah More who was a pioneer in the provision of education for children from less privileged families.

More information about any of these ministries or the residential conference facilities available in this historic estate can be seen on the linked websites of www.the-park.net, or by contacting any of the ministry offices at Moggerhanger Park, Bedford, MK 44 3RW,

The Centre for Contemporary Ministry

CCM, one of the founding ministries, had its teaching and training base at Bawtry Hall in Yorkshire. Its ministry originally was primarily in offering in-service training courses for clergy in pastoral charge with consultations on theological issues. Since coming to Moggerhanger it has widened its courses and conferences ministry to include teaching on prophecy and church growth, which were the focus of the two other founding ministries Prophetic Word Ministries and the British Church Growth Association.

Pardes, The Centre for Biblical and Hebraic Studies

Pardes (Hebrew for 'The Park') was originally part of PWM's ministry. It explores the Hebrew origins of the Gospel and the Christian faith.

Family Matters Institute

FMI, founded by the CCM gives support to church leaders in a time of rapid social change. The Institute has produced a number of research reports which have been published in association with the Parliamentary Family and Child Protection Group. Its ministry includes parenting courses, family debt counselling and a range of family and marriage resources.

21st Century Clapham Connections

Clapham Connections, established in 2000, builds on the spiritual heritage of Moggerhanger House, its connections with the Thornton family, William Wilberforce and the Clapham Sect whose work in the 18th century changed the course of history. Its ministry is to initiate similar movements to bring Christian values into the 21st-century life. It is involved in the 'Set All Free' commemoration of the 200th anniversary of the Abolition of the Slave Trade in 2007.

Christian Workplace Forum

CWF, founded in 2003, aims to enable Christians in the Workplace to be more effective in personal witness and in changing the institutions in which they work. Links have been established with some 85 Christian associations in the professions, commerce and industry. Links have also been established with the student world through UCCF to encourage students to take their faith into the workplace.

Transform-uk

Transform-uk aims to transform the spiritual life of the nation by emphasising biblical values. It has the support of main-line churches and is led by a core group from 'Clapham Connections' and the 'Christian Workplace Forum'. It aims to impact the UK with strategic, God-directed campaigns over the next 40 years.

Healthy Church UK

Healthy Church UK is the successor to the British Church Growth Association and seeks to work with local churches to find and encourage the best practice for improving the health and growth of local churches. It publishes a quarterly magazine He@lthyChurch.mag.uk, and carries out surveys and consultations on Natural Church Development.

C & M Ministries

C&M Ministries is a small trust specifically set up to provide support for the wider ministry of Clifford and Monica Hill, particularly their ministry in Africa and the Far East and overseas study tours such as the one that led to this book. The trust also administers the publication and distribution of a bimonthly *'State of the Nation'* Update Tape recorded by Cliff as well as promoting and distributing all the books they have both written.

Moggerhanger House Preservation Trust

An important part of the Moggerhanger Park family is the Moggerhanger House Preservation Trust. The trust was set up in 1997 to carry out the restoration of the premises and the estate. All the ministries owe an enormous debt of gratitude to the Trustees of MHPT who have shown great commitment and dedication in raising funds and overseeing the restoration of the house and grounds.

Moggerhanger Park Ltd

MP Ltd has been established specifically by MHPT to operate the Moggerhanger House and estate. Its staff carry the responsibility for organising the day-to-day activities, for opening the house and estate to the public at certain times of the year, for running the tea rooms and most importantly providing the resources for the ministries' use of the house. They work closely with all the ministries, especially from October to June each year when the house is open as a Christian Conference Centre.

Contents of CD

Individual Diji album files for each of the seven churches of Revelation:

Ephesus   **Smyrna**   **Pergamum**   **Thyatira**
Sardis   **Philadelphia**   **Laodicea**

Also Diji album files of four other places of interest in the area:

Colossae   **Hierapolis**   **Miletus**   **Didyma**

A further Diji album of **Modern Turkey**

Microsoft Powerpoint Presentations (ppt) and shows (pps), with user notes and handouts:

1 Seven Churches of Revelation
2 Ancient and Modern

Diji Album Viewer Instructions

This software package has been made available to us

1 Double click on the file name that corresponds to one of the seven churches of Revelation (eg Sardis).

2 Diji viewer will automatically open showing the Welcome to Diji Album Viewer screen and giving the six main icons needed to operate the viewer. These are self-explanatory.

3 Click on "close" to see the album - example below.

4 The albums have been built with a maximum of four images per page with brief titles for each image.

5 A small-scale thumbnail page index is shown on the left-hand side of the screen to allow for quick and easy assess to a page of your choice.

6 The six main icons can also be used to display the album pages in the mode of your choice.

7 Selected album pages can also be printed or sent as e-mail attachments.

8 The individual image files (as compressed jpg files) are found in individual directories with the same file names as displayed in the album pages. These can be used in your own presentations (see copyright comment in the ReadMeFile in this CD.